Gaining
the Systems
Advantage

STRATEGIES TO ELIMINATE STRESS,
WORK FEWER HOURS,
AND BE MORE PROFITABLE IN YOUR BUSINESS

DARYL MURROW

Crescendo
PUBLISHING

Gaining the Systems Advantage: Strategies to Eliminate Stress, Work Fewer Hours, and Be More Profitable in Your Business
By Daryl Murrow

Crescendo Publishing, LLC
300 Carlsbad Village Drive
Ste. 108A, #443
Carlsbad, California 92008-2999
GetPublished@CrescendoPublishing.com
1-877-575-8814

ISBN: 978-1-944177-81-2 (p)
ISBN: 978-1-944177-82-9 (e)

Printed in the United States of America
Cover design by BDTK studio

10 9 8 7 6 5 4 3 2 1

A Gift from the Author

Accompanying this book is the complete set of FREE tools for implementing the strategies to help you transform your business. These tools are the perfect companion to the book, and they are yours for free.

Download them at www.darylmurrow.com/toolkit

Testimonials

"Are you ready to own your business instead of your business owning you? We recommend this book to anyone who is looking at ways to eliminate chaos, successfully work on your business and have the success you dreamed of when you started this journey. This book does an excellent job opening your eyes to the solutions you are seeking for the problems you're facing in your business. We wish we would have had this information years ago!"

Josh & Alicia Burns, Owners
Total Lawn Care of Olympia

"If you're wanting your business to be more organized and efficient, then you need to read this book!"

Joshua McCarty, CEO
Mint Landscapes, LLC

"Daryl's book Gaining the Systems Advantage is a fantastic resource for business owners. He shares easy to apply tools that you can put together immediately to take your business to the next level."

Jason Phillips, Founder & President
Zoe Juice Bar

"This book provides a powerful, practical, and simple set of tools for running your business. A must read for any business owner and their management team."

Kevin Leneker, CEO
Single Handed Consulting

Table of Contents

INTRODUCTION 5

TOOLS FOR GAINING CLARITY 9
    CHAPTER 1 - CONQUER THE PLATEAU EFFECT 11
    CHAPTER 2 - TAKE TOTAL RESPONSIBILITY 17
    CHAPTER 3 - BECOME THE "NEW CEO" OF YOUR BUSINESS 27
    CHAPTER 4 - DEFINE YOUR PERSONAL SUCCESS 35

TOOLS FOR SETTING DIRECTION 41
    CHAPTER 5 - CREATE YOUR IDEAL BUSINESS VISION 43
    CHAPTER 6 - IDENTIFY YOUR CORE VALUES 51
    CHAPTER 7 - UNDERSTAND YOUR MISSION 59

TOOLS FOR ORGANIZING YOUR WORK 65
    CHAPTER 8 - DETERMINE WHAT NEEDS TO BE DONE 67
    CHAPTER 9 - ASSIGN WORK ACCOUNTABILITIES 79
    CHAPTER 10 - CLARIFY EMPLOYEE EXPECTATIONS 89

TOOLS FOR GETTING YOUR WORK DONE 99
    CHAPTER 11 - HARNESS THE POWER OF SYSTEMS 101
    CHAPTER 12 - DEVELOP REFERENCE MANUALS 115
    CHAPTER 13 - MONITOR YOUR VITAL SIGNS 125
    CHAPTER 14 - IMPROVE EMPLOYEE RELATIONSHIPS 135

PUTTING IT ALL TOGETHER
    CHAPTER 15 - EMBRACE THE CHANGE 145
    CHAPTER 16 - NEXT STEPS 153

Dedication

To anyone courageous enough to launch your own business, may your business always be fun, rewarding, and profitable!

Acknowledgements

There are so many people to thank for helping this book become a reality. I'm where I am today because of the people I've met and the friendships I've made over the years. For those that helped educate me, believed in me, supported me, influenced me, and somehow shaped me into the person I've become, I'm forever grateful.

La Donna Murrow, Gary Murrow, Candace Murrow, Tracy Larson, Jeff Murrow, Lyle Murrow, Joe Murrow, Andrew Murrow, Ginger Alva, Brian Tracy, L Perry Wilbur, Michael Gerber, Charles Givens, Dean Jones, Carla Jones, Craig Jones, Tom Lawrence, Michael Cade, Celia Nightingale, Ron Nielsen, Margi Kenny, Kathy Perciful, Lisa Smith, Beth Oppliger, Joanne Lee, Cheryl Brown, Shirley Smith-Moore, George Sharp, Patrick Snow, Kieran Murry, Sarah Victory, Dale Kershner, Robbin Simons, Shayna Rohrig, Kevin Leneker, Jason Phillips, Ronald Remmel, and all the folks at the Thurston EDC.

My beautiful and supportive wife, who continues to stand by me every step of the way, Raquel Chin-Quee Murrow.

To all my clients—past, present, and future—you're absolutely amazing! Your hard work and dedication to building an incredible business truly inspire me. It's such a privilege to work with you.

Introduction

If you're a business owner with employees and you feel overwhelmed, frustrated, or unhappy with your business, I wrote this book especially for you.

I know you've worked very hard in your business to get it where it is today. You've sacrificed a lot, worked long hours, and paid your dues. However, deep inside you know there's more to business than what you're currently experiencing. You know there's another level—you just haven't reached it yet.

The joy and satisfaction you used to experience in your business have probably been replaced by one or all the following frustrations:

- A lack of effectiveness – You feel frustrated, stuck, or overwhelmed. Issues constantly seem to appear from out of nowhere. You want to make changes, but you're not sure which ones are the right changes to make.

- Lack of cash flow – You run out of cash at the most critical times and aren't sure what's happening to all the cash coming in, or where it disappeared to at the end of the month.

- Issues with employees – You have a difficult time getting your employees to respect you and do what you're paying them to do.

- Not enough quality time off – You work far more hours than you want to; at times, you feel like your business owns you instead of the other way around. You dream of being able to take a quality vacation again.

- Chaos and dysfunction – Whatever you try to do doesn't seem to work. You feel as if you're treading water and not making any real progress. Things always seem to go wrong at the worst possible time.

In a growing business, these are quite common, predictable frustrations. If you're not experiencing any of these, you're definitely in the minority.

In the early 1990s I opened my first retail store. Like most entrepreneurs I know, I jumped headfirst into this business despite my lack of both prior experience and the necessary skills required to run a successful business. Everything I did was completely through trial and error.

As the business began to grow and started to gain some success, I did what seemed natural: I opened a second location. If one store was doing well, I reasoned, opening a second store was sure to double my amount of success. I couldn't have been more wrong. Do you know what did double? The number of problems and the amount of stress I had.

It seemed like every time I attempted to expand and grow, my problems compounded even more. With every new problem I faced, I felt the happiness slowly draining out of me.

It got so bad that I was stressed out, frustrated, and usually angry on a daily basis. In fact, I refer to this period of my life as the "Angry Daryl" phase. Our operations were extremely inefficient, and I had a difficult time managing our employees. I was consumed with a burning desire to make the business run better, yet I really didn't know how to do it.

Eventually, all I was doing was putting out fires all day long. It never failed. There was always an issue that needed my attention—from employees, vendors, or customers.

This stress and anxiety threw me into depression. My business felt like it was sucking the life out of me. I had created a monster, and I didn't know how to break free from it. I no longer liked going in to work; some days I stayed in bed the entire day, as if I was paralyzed.

Then one day my life forever changed when I discovered there was a better way to organize, operate, and manage my business. As I began to implement these changes into the business, one by one my frustrations began to disappear, and I experienced a dramatic transformation that resulted in a new kind of freedom. I no longer had to work fifty to sixty hours per week. I no longer had to go in to work each day if I didn't want to. I was finally free to pursue other things I wanted to do.

In 2008 I sold the business and started helping stressed-out, overwhelmed, frustrated business owners organize, operate, and manage their businesses in a whole new way. A way that worked for them.

Most of my clients are small to mid-size companies ($1 million to $10 million in revenue with 5–50 employees) that are growth-oriented and willing to change, to be open-minded, and to listen. If this describes you, then perhaps you're ready to transform your business and experience. You already have everything you need to be successful.

To Your SUCCESS,

Daryl Murrow

MODULE ONE:

TOOLS FOR GAINING CLARITY

"I used to blame my problems on other people. But my moment of clarity, if you want to call it that, came when I was looking in the mirror one day and just burst into tears. It wasn't just that I looked bad, it was that I knew my problem was me."
- Tom Sizemore

Several years ago, I started having difficulty reading small print. Although I was aware of the problem, I ignored it until straining my eyes no longer helped. My eyesight was getting worse, and I had to do something about it.

I decided to start wearing contact lenses and was shocked when I realized how easily I could now see the small print. It was as if I'd been looking through a blurry telescope and was now able to focus the lens. As excited as I was about this new level of clarity, I was shocked by how much I really couldn't see before.

I designed the first three chapters of this book to help you focus on yourself as the leader of your business, to gain a whole new level of clarity about how you might be holding yourself back, and what you can do to move yourself forward. Like putting on a new set of glasses, you'll begin to see things you've never seen before. If you're open to what you might discover, let the journey begin.

CHAPTER 1

CONQUER THE PLATEAU EFFECT

"We live within this reality we create, and we're quite unaware of how we create the reality."
- James Turrell

If your business has continued to grow steadily over the past several years, you probably have more work than you can handle and even far more problems to deal with. You work hard to get things under control, only to have a new issue develop. Whether it's dealing with employees, satisfying your customers, or trying to prevent the next catastrophe, there's no shortage of things you have to deal with. Without even being aware of it, you've been caught in the plateau effect!

The plateau effect captures unsuspecting business owners, entangling them in a state of organizational chaos and dysfunction. Because you're reading this book, it's likely you're caught in the plateau effect now.

The plateau effect occurs when a business grows, expanding at a faster pace than the business owner's skills and capacity can handle. When a business is small, the owner often does all the work themselves, and they do the work in their business the way they want to. They're in complete control and call all the shots. Everything relies on the business owner. If the owner happens to be away and a question arises, the employees will call the owner to ask what to do.

This scenario is okay when the business is small, but as the business expands and adds employees, the owner is going to be asked more and more questions, getting pulled in multiple directions—not to mention all the customer interactions the owner has to handle. It doesn't take long for the owner's capacity to get used up.

In addition to maxing out the owner's capacity, a growing business requires additional skills that most owners don't have. In fact, most business owners are unaware that these additional skills are required as the business grows, so as the business grows, the owner is usually unequipped to handle that growth.

UNCONSCIOUS INCOMPETENCE

When I started my business, I lacked any type of formal training. Inspired by one business book I had read, I thought my dedication, hard work, and perseverance would be enough to help me succeed in business. I've always been a fast learner and believed I could figure out everything I needed. It wasn't until years later that I realized I was truly an unconscious incompetent: I didn't know what I didn't know.

I was pretty ignorant. I lacked any real comprehension about the different skill sets needed to organize, operate, and manage a business, let alone a successful business.

I approached everything with a trial-and-error mentality, but looking back now, I really wasn't prepared when the business started to grow and my workload expanded with it.

At first, I started working long hours and taking less time off, but eventually it became next to impossible to accomplish what I used to be able to get done in a normal day. To alleviate the workload, I started hiring employees. I certainly wasn't prepared for this. I had no idea what I was getting into, and I ended up with a lot of additional issues and problems to worry about.

Eventually I found myself spending most of my time dealing with problems and feeling overwhelmed, overworked, and stressed out because of all the things I had to do. I was caught in the plateau effect and couldn't escape.

Interestingly enough, from the outside, things didn't look too bad. We had great products, and we provided excellent customer service. We were profitable and looked successful. However, I continually felt as if I was spinning my wheels.

A company can remain on a plateau for a very long time, if the owner is still calling the shots. One time I was brought in to see if I could help a company that was having difficulties getting things under control. This company had close to fifty employees and had been in business for twenty-five years, so I was really curious about what kind of help they would need. To my surprise, the entire company was heavily reliant on the founder and CEO. Although he had established different departments with their own managers, the CEO still called all the shots in all areas of the company. His capacity was completely maxed out, and he'd been running his company this way for years. It wasn't until he started thinking about retirement that he realized the company might fall apart if he left.

On the other hand, companies avoid the plateau effect by remaining very small. I know such a business that's been around for nearly thirty years. It's comprised of a husband-and-wife team who have never once hired an employee. When they go on vacation, they hang a sign on the door. Staying this size made them feel very comfortable and happy, and it kept them out of the plateau effect.

THERE'S NO NEED TO SUFFER

I hope you now have a good idea of what the plateau effect is, but even with that understanding, you might not know how to conquer it once and for all. How can you organize, operate, and manage your business in a way that works the way you want it to?

You want to create a company:

- Where everyone is clear about the work they're supposed to do and the outcomes they're accountable for producing
- Where everyone is properly trained on how to do their work
- Where people actually like coming into work, and where everybody feels like they're on the same page
- That can function without you having to be there, allowing you the time off and vacations you deserve without any catastrophes awaiting your return

To conquer the plateau effect, you must become aware of the new skills and knowledge that can help you keep pace with the growth of your business and then make the necessary changes.

Awareness is the first step. Once you begin moving forward by using the tools outlined in this book, you'll never look back. I didn't.

Making this investment in yourself and in your business is by no means a quick-fix solution. The larger the business, the longer it's going to take. However, the strategies you learn in this book will work for you, as they've worked for hundreds of others. As long you're patient and are willing to do the work, you really can experience the freedom you're looking for.

These are the only questions left: Are you truly ready to make the commitment? Are you ready to commit to conquering the plateau effect once and for all? Are you ready to start eliminating the stress, the feeling of being overwhelmed, and the dysfunction experienced in your business? If so, let's get started!

SUMMARY

- The plateau effect catches unsuspecting business owners in a state of organizational chaos, causing stress and the feelings of being overwhelmed and constantly out of control.

- Most small business owners are unconsciously incompetent when it comes to growing their business. They don't know what they don't know. As a business grows and expands its number of employees, additional skills and knowledge are required.

- The only way to conquer the plateau effect is to invest in yourself to increase your knowledge and skill level to keep pace with the growth of your business, and to limit how much your employees have to depend on you to make all the decisions in the business.

CHAPTER 2

TAKE TOTAL RESPONSIBILITY

*"If you could kick the person in the pants
responsible for most of your trouble,
you wouldn't sit for a month."*
- Theodore Roosevelt

In the first chapter we discussed the plateau effect and how it snares unsuspecting business owners. We also talked about how conquering the plateau effect requires a commitment to working on yourself. The first step in making this commitment is taking total responsibility.

Taking total responsibility means that no matter what happens in your business, you're responsible for it. It doesn't matter how big or small the issue is, or if you intentionally created it in the first place. The fact remains that you—and you alone—are ultimately responsible for the fact that it happened, along with everything else that happens in your business—everything!

For some people, the concept of taking total responsibility is hard to take. They have a difficult time accepting this as reality. However, until you accept responsibility for everything that happens in your business, you'll have a difficult time implementing the tools outlined in this book, eliminating your frustrations, and bringing about the needed change you desire.

In an effort to avoid taking total responsibility for their business, an owner will often change their personality as some type of coping mechanism, which can be quite detrimental to the overall health of a business. There are two common types of adopted personalities. I refer to them as the victim and the ostrich.

THE VICTIM

The victim is an individual who, no matter what happens to them, refuses to accept responsibility for the things that happen to them and would rather blame someone or something else for all their problems. Because they always blame somebody or something else, the victim never feels like they're in control; therefore, they can do very little to find solutions for their problems.

Being a victim and not taking responsibility for your business are extremely counterproductive behaviors and can severely limit your growth. Nobody likes a complainer, and people won't want to help you. Here are a few things to check to make sure you haven't adopted a victim mentality.

YOU BLAME OTHER PEOPLE

If you find yourself getting upset and blaming others on a regular basis, you're probably living like a victim.

- Are you constantly annoyed by your employees? Do you get upset at them for the things they're doing or not doing?
- Do your vendors or contractors upset you?
- Do you have customers that push your hot buttons and upset you?

- Do you regularly tell your complaints to other people, such as your friends and family?

Sure, some people may intentionally do terrible things to us. Maybe they have some personal reason to behave this way. However, in most cases the reason an issue arises in the first place is that we allowed it to happen. If employees aren't doing things the way you want them to, the cause might be your training, your systems, or the way they're held accountable.

Your accountant might be in error because they didn't file your taxes on time, but filing taxes on time is your overall responsibility, not theirs, and you're responsible for hiring them in the first place. If you're mad at a customer because they misunderstood one of your policies, perhaps your policies need to be rewritten. No matter what the circumstance, you allowed this to happen in the first place. It's your responsibility.

WANT SOME CHEESE WITH THAT WHINE?

Many years ago, I was working alongside several of my employees when another employee walked by and said, "Wah, wah, wah." Caught off guard, I turned and said, "Excuse me?" Once again, he said, "Wah, wah, wah." When I asked why he said that, he told me it was because I was whining. "You're whining again, Daryl. You sound like a big whining baby."

As I processed what my employee had just said to me, I was completely shocked that he had the nerve to actually call me out. I also realized that he was right. I was a whiner, and in those days, that was the norm. I was acting like a victim who complained about everything: sales weren't high enough, employees weren't doing their jobs correctly, certain customers were being unreasonable. It didn't matter what the situation was because I always had some valid reason to complain about it.

Without even being aware of it, I had developed a habit of blaming my problems on my employees. Being called out as a whiner turned out to be a wonderful gift from that employee. It gave me chance to look at my actions and motives. It gave me an opportunity to stop thinking of myself as a helpless victim of circumstance and to start taking total responsibility for EVERYTHING that was happening inside my business.

YOU BLAME SITUATIONS

Do you find yourself blaming the economy, changes in the industry, increased competition, or any other situation for your business's performance? Are you judgmental and constantly critical of things around you? It's easy to blame situations that seem out of our control because it allows us to try to remove our own responsibility from what's happening in our business. However, this puts us directly in the middle of the victim category.

Because your business is constantly evolving and changing, it's your responsibility to change and adapt with it. If you catch yourself blaming outside situations for issues you're facing in your business, stop and ask yourself, "What have I done, or not done, that allowed this to happen in my business?" You may not like the answer, but at least you're taking total responsibility.

YOU BELIEVE THINGS ARE UNFAIR

If you ever catch yourself saying that something's unfair, you're living as a victim instead of taking total responsibility. *Why do all these things happen to me? Why can't I ever get a break? Why do I always get beat up? This is so unfair.* If you're talking to yourself in this manner, using these types of words, then chances are you're living your life as a victim. Deciding whether something is fair or unfair implies you're the victim of outside circumstances that are happening to you. Sure, plenty of things can happen that we may not expect, but how we choose to respond to them can mean the difference between taking responsibility or feeling like a victim.

THE OSTRICH

The ostrich is an individual who operates their business and makes daily decisions as if their head was buried in the sand. Because of this, they have no idea how their business is performing. They don't understand how to read their financial statements or project their cash flow, and nothing is really being measured or analyzed in their business.

Because the ostrich is oblivious to what's truly happening inside their business, an ostrich will often make decisions without understanding the full impact of their decision, leading to a higher probability of making costly mistakes. In addition, they're often unsure what needs to be done and what should be their priority.

The ostrich is a serious danger to themselves. They don't realize that the light at the end of the tunnel is really a train heading straight toward them.

BUSINESS IS GREAT!

The other day I ran into a business owner I know and asked him, "How's business going?"

"Business is great!" he answered enthusiastically. He then paused and said, "But I haven't updated my accounting since the beginning of the year." Since it was now November, I was quite stunned.

"Then how do you know you're doing great if you haven't updated your accounting?" I asked.

"Well, our daily POS sales reports shows our sales are much higher than last year." Shocking! However, before I could respond, he told me, "My wife did have to take $5,000 from her personal account and put it into the business so we could pay taxes."

I never asked him why he hadn't bothered to update his accounting program, but I'm sure he had a really good excuse. This guy had absolutely no idea how his business was performing. He had no idea how much money he was making, what his expenses were, or how much profit he was making. Unfortunately, this is far more common than one might expect.

I run into business owners on a regular basis who have adopted the ostrich mentality. For some, I think it's just too painful for them to see how their business is really performing. If this describes you, then you owe it to yourself, your employees, and your customers to pull your head out of the sand, become aware, and start paying attention to what's happening all around you. As with anything else, the more you practice, the better you become.

BECOME SOLUTION-ORIENTED

Becoming solution-oriented means you focus on finding a solution instead of focusing on the problem. Even though you're going to take total responsibility for everything that happens in your business and stop complaining and blaming others, your problems aren't going to miraculously disappear. Things that irritate and frustrate you are still going to happen, but taking a solutions approach enables you to look at what's upsetting you in a different light.

WHAT'S THE PROBLEM?

Problems that irritate you are actually opportunities in disguise because they usually indicate something needs to be fixed or developed. When we accept responsibility and don't blame others, we can look for the root cause of the problem.

If we can do this and leave our emotions out of it, we become solution-oriented. When put into practice, you'll find it much easier over time to solve your problems while keeping your stress level under control.

To take total responsibility and become solution-oriented, you need to look for the root cause of your problems, starting with one problem that really irritates you. Perhaps it's something that you've been putting up with that keeps recurring.

1. Identify the problem. Write down this irritating problem and the frustration it causes you.

2. Write down what you believe is causing this problem. Remember not to place any blame. when you dig deeper, you can find the root cause. If an employee keeps making a mistake, why does that keep happening? Have they been properly trained? Is a procedure missing? Is a policy not in place? Keep asking yourself questions until you find the root cause of the problem.

3. Identify the solution. Write down what it would take to fix the problem, even if you're not exactly sure how to make it happen. Perhaps one of your irritating problems is that you keep running out of important office supplies. Instead of blaming your employee, you realize the solution would be to develop a better inventory-control system, maybe one that can identify when supplies need to be reordered. You've identified that you need an inventory-control system, but you might not know at this time how to develop one. At least you've determined the solution, and you can stop placing the blame.

IT'S JUST AN EVENT

Many years ago, I was introduced to the concept that really helped me to stop blaming others and getting upset. The concept is actually quite simple: life is just a series of events.

Life is just a series of events, and everything that happens to you is just an event. Events happen one after another, but each one of these events is actually 100 percent neutral. It's only when we experience an event that we decide if we're going to turn it into a positive or negative event. It's always our choice.

Taking total responsibility means you recognize events when they occur for what they are and keep them in perspective. Negative things don't just happen to you. Things happen to you, and you chose to see them as negative. Whenever you're faced with an unpleasant situation, simply remember, "This is just an event."

It's your Choice

Are you ready to take total responsibility in your life? Good. Then you need to take an honest assessment of yourself to see if you blame people and situations for your problems. I wasn't aware I was a whiner until somebody brought it to my attention. Is it time to pull your head out of the sand and start paying attention to your business? At the end of the day, it's all up to you; nobody's going to force you. It's your choice. Identify and resolve to give up any negative habits you're aware of that may be impacting your business.

Key Points

- Taking total responsibility for your life and business means no matter what happens in your business, you take responsibility for it happening in the first place.

- A victim blames other people and situations for all their problems, rather than taking total responsibility for their life and business.

- An ostrich is unware of what's really happening in their business. They operate their business as if their head is stuck in the sand, causing them to focus their attention in the wrong areas of their business.

- Problems that irritate you are always going to happen. Instead of placing the blame, look to discover the root cause of every problem, and find a solution.

- Life is just a series of neutral events. You decide whether you want them to be negative or positive.

ACTION STEPS

1. Do you act like a victim? List all the circumstances you can think of in which you have NOT taken total responsibility and have blamed someone or something else for your problems.

2. Write a list of every problem that irritates you. Let's get the list down on paper.

3. Identify the root causes of these irritating problems you might be currently facing, and see if you can find solutions to them.

4. Are you an ostrich? With your head buried in the sand, what important things are you ignoring in your business?

Chapter 3

Become the "New CEO" of Your Business

"Great CEOs are not just born with shiny hair and a tie."
- Marc Andreessen

In the last chapter we discussed the importance of taking total responsibility for everything in your business. We also talked about two personality types, the victim and the ostrich, that might be holding you back. It's now time to step up and focus on becoming the true leader of your business.

We already discussed the fact that most people start a business without any formal business training. If this describes you, then technically, you assumed the role of CEO by default the day you opened your business, and you've been working very hard in that role ever since. However, you still might be wearing many hats on a daily basis and performing most of the work that has to be done in the business.

Maybe it never occurred to you that by wearing all the different hats and performing all of these different tasks, you created a job for yourself. There's a big difference between a business owner who works in the business all day long, and a business owner who doesn't have to come into work. The difference is that if you're working all day long in your business, you really own a job.

To make the desired changes in your business that are outlined in this book, you need to formalize the relationship you have with your business.

IT'S TIME FOR A PROMOTION!

Because changing your business requires starting at the top, it's important to start with the view you have of yourself and your business. No longer are you going to be the person that does everything in your business. No longer are you going to be caught up in the daily frustrations without any plan for getting out of them. No longer are you going to drift aimlessly or feel stuck in your business. You're not going to let that happen because it's time to give yourself a promotion and become the "NEW CEO" of your business.

According to the definition on Investopedia.com:

A **chief executive officer** (**CEO**) is the highest-ranking **executive** in a company, whose main responsibilities include:

- Development and implementation of high-level strategies
- Making major (corporate) decisions
- Managing the overall operations and resources of a company
- Acting as the main point of communication between the board of directors and the corporate operations

Notice that nowhere in this definition does it say the CEO cleans the toilet, packages the products, fixes the machinery, or undertakes all the daily activities of the business.

THINKING STRATEGICALLY

As the NEW CEO of your business, it's time to shift your priorities for your business with a strategic focus. Becoming a strategic leader means you're responsible for leading the company to reach its vision.

Strategic leadership means being proactive instead of reactive by taking deliberate, intentional action. Strategic leadership involves planning: identifying and working through the steps required to lead your business to your desired destination, tracking the plan on a consistent basis, monitoring and measuring progress, and making corrections along the way.

Becoming a NEW CEO and strategic leader requires you to step outside the day-to-day business and view your business from a 10,000-foot level instead. Michael Gerber, author of *The E-Myth Revisited*, describes this concept in detail as the difference between "working ON instead of IN your business."

WORKING IN YOUR BUSINESS

The majority of small business owners spend their time working IN their business. Working IN your business leads to the Plateau Effect. It refers to doing all the daily work that gets done in your business: making sure the clients are taken care of, the phone calls and emails get answered, and the accounting is updated. It's the frantic pace of the daily hustle and bustle. You work hard all day long and seem busier than ever, but this type of work usually doesn't do much to help you reach your vision.

A business owner can get stuck in the Plateau Effect working IN their business for a very long time, which often leads to burnout. When problems and frustrations start to arise, working IN your business is often described as treading water—doing lots of activity but not really going anywhere.

WORKING ON YOUR BUSINESS

On the other hand, working ON your business refers to working on the growth and development of your business. It's the process that enables you to view, assess, and establish the future direction of your business. Working ON your business is creating the vision for what you want your business to become in the future, the goals and objectives you want to reach, and the action plan for the steps you'll take to get there. Working ON your business is how growth happens. Working ON your business can eventually free you from working IN your business. It's an investment in your future and deserves the highest priority.

WHAT IS WORKING IN YOUR BUSINESS COSTING YOU?

Another way to compare working IN your business and working ON your business is to look at what your work is costing you. You may have thought about it before, but the time you spend working IN your business has a price tag, your hourly rate. If you work fifty weeks per year on average and forty hours each week, this means you work roughly 2,000 hours per year. When you divide your yearly salary by 2,000, you can determine your hourly rate:

- $50,000 / 2,000 = $25 per hour
- $75,000 / 2,000 = $37.50 per hour
- $100,000 / 2,000 = $50 per hour

If you were to list all the mundane tasks you do on a weekly basis, you could add up the number of hours it takes to complete them, multiply them by your hourly rate, and get a true reflection of what these tasks are costing you to do each week.

If the real-world cost to do a task is less than your hourly rate, somebody else should be doing the job. Every hour spent working IN is one hour less you can spend working ON your business. The natural tendency is to do the work yourself to save money, but paying to have this work done is really an investment in your future, not an expense; it's an investment in achieving your most important goals.

TIME IS OUR MOST PRECIOUS RESOURCE

Time is the only resource you can't get back; it's far more valuable than money. How you use your time is up to you.

Make a list of all your mundane tasks, and take a minute to calculate your hourly rate. Pay others to do things for you that cost less than what it would cost for you to do them. Free up as much time to work on the activities that have the highest payoff and that lead you to your most important goals and the things you value most. If your goals and spending time with people you value are truly the most important things in your life, why would you want to spend time on anything else?

YOU HAVE TO MAKE THE TIME TO WORK ON YOUR BUSINESS

Most business owners tell me they're too busy working IN their business to work ON their business. "I just don't have any time" or "I'm too worn out and exhausted doing all the things I have to do" are the responses I usually hear.

Unfortunately, the only way to conquer the Plateau Effect and find the time to work ON your business is to make the time, and as the NEW CEO of your business, this is your responsibility.

Taking time to do this type of strategically focused work is a serious investment in your future that will pay great dividends over time. Similar to saving money, if you don't pay yourself first, there will never be enough money left over to pay anybody else.

I remember the first time I learned this concept and was eager to start working ON my business. I was working so many long hours and had so many other commitments that I had difficulty finding even one free hour. I started small and began investing one hour of my weekend to work ON my business. I created a weekly appointment on my calendar and called it "Work ON Business."

As I began to spend more and more time doing this strategic work, I started to add extra hours whenever I could. Eventually it became a routine I enjoyed that produced positive results over time.

Are you ready to be strategic and start working ON your business instead of IN your business? Are you committed to finding a few extra hours per week and marking "Work ON Business" on your calendar?

Nobody will ever make this time for you—and you'll never have enough time. So make it happen, and start taking serious action.

KEY POINTS

- Up until now, you've really owned a job. Now it's time to promote yourself to the NEW CEO of your business. Your primary responsibility is to be the strategic leader of your company.

- Working IN your business involves doing all the work that makes your business run on a daily basis. Every task you do while working IN your business has a cost. Make sure you're not doing work that would cost less if somebody else did the work.

- Working ON your business means you're working on activities that lead to the growth and development of your business. As the NEW CEO of your business, working ON your business deserves your highest priority.

ACTION STEPS

1. Write out a list of all the activities you do in your business. Identify which activities are considered working IN your business versus working ON your business.

2. Calculate how much it costs you to do the activities when working IN your business.

3. Set aside some time to start "Working ON Business." It's up to you to make the time. The work will never get done if you don't schedule it on your calendar.

CHAPTER 4

DEFINE YOUR PERSONAL SUCCESS

*"A man is a success if he gets up in the
morning and gets to bed at night, and in
between he does what he wants to do."*
- Bob Dylan

In the last chapter, we discussed the idea of you becoming the NEW CEO of your business, and now it's time to handle your first responsibility: making a major decision. It's time to clarify exactly what you want your business to become and to lead the company to achieve it.

However, before you define what you want your business to become in the next few years, you should define what success means to you. We all seem to strive for success, yet we all seem to have different interpretations of what success means to us. What does success really mean to you?

DEFINE YOUR VERSION OF SUCCESS

Many people believe success is about having a lot of money, status, fame, competition, power, or possessions. However, we've all seen examples of people who, on the outside, looked like they'd achieved a great deal of success, but on the inside felt empty and unsatisfied.

Defining your success can and should include material things, but it should also include something much deeper, something that means much more. Being a success should mean that you're living a life that's authentic and true to yourself, one that's in alignment with your values, feeds your desires, and is fueled by your passion. A life that's truly meaningful and emotionally gratifying to you. A life that you want to live versus a life that you have to live. A life you feel like you're living on your terms.

Your own personal definition of success can act as a filter for the important decisions that you make and can prevent you from striving to achieve things that leave you feeling unfulfilled and unsatisfied. It can help you engage in activities and set goals that really matter, and it can let you know when you achieve it.

When you clearly understand what your personal definition of success means to you, you're able to live your life with intention, instead of randomly drifting along. When you clarify what you want, you can make clear choices that are in alignment with what's most important to you. It helps you set your life's priorities and puts your business in perspective.

DON'T ACCEPT ANYBODY ELSE'S VERSION OF SUCCESS

Sometimes we adopt a version of success that we picked up from somebody else while we were growing up. We accepted this version as our own and might even still believe it to be our own. For some people, reaching a certain net worth means they're successful; for others, success might mean doing work they truly love each day. You owe it to yourself to discover what makes you want to fly out of bed each day. One of my favorite quotes is from Steve Jobs:

"Your work is going to fill a large part of your life, and the only way to be truly satisfied is to do what you believe is great work. And the only way to do great work is to love what you do. If you haven't found it yet, keep looking. Don't settle. As with all matters of the heart, you'll know when you find it."

Since we all know time is limited, it's important that we take the time to make sure we're pursuing our version of success—not somebody else's.

DON'T LET YOUR BUSINESS CONSUME YOUR LIFE

Your business should provide a means to help you achieve what you really want out of life, but many business owners instead feel as if their life's been consumed by their business.

I can remember a time when I was so overwhelmed in my business that I felt like I'd created a monster. I'd become so consumed by my business, and I didn't know how to handle it. I remember wondering how I was ever going to get out from under it.

Can you remember why you started your business in the first place? Whatever the reason, you probably started your business because you were looking for a way to make your life better. Perhaps it was to increase your income, do things your way, or have the freedom and flexibility to be your own boss. I'm quite positive you didn't start your business so that you could work all the time.

Defining your own version of success can help you keep things in perspective and make sure that your business won't demand your time away from the things that really matter to you, that it will give you the time instead.

Take the time to examine and clarify what you really want to achieve. Once you're able to define your own version of success, you'll be more satisfied with your business over the long term.

DEFINING YOUR EXIT STRATEGY

You may have no desire to exit your business in the near future, but that doesn't mean you shouldn't define an exit for yourself. Sometime in the future, you're not going to want to keep doing your business. There are many reasons for this, such as retirement, illness, relocation, or you just get bored.

Do you want to pass your business to your children, sell the business to your employees (or to somebody else), or simply sell everything off and shut it down? Deciding on your exit strategy now will save you time later and keep you in alignment with your own personal version of success.

KEY POINTS

- Take the time to define what success means to you. Your business should be designed to help you achieve this success you desire, not consume your life.

- Your version of success belongs to you; there is no right or wrong version. Beware of adopting somebody else's version of success.

- Sometime in the future, you may not want to be in business. Take the time to define your exit strategy so that you're prepared.

ACTION STEPS

1. Define your own personal version of success. Become clear about what success means to you.
   a. What truly excites you?
   b. What would you like to have more of in your life?
   c. What would you like to have less of or eliminate from your life?
   d. How do you want to feel each day at work?

e. How do you define success for your business?

f. What does success mean to you?

2. Define an exit strategy for your business. When do you want to exit and how?

MODULE TWO:

TOOLS FOR SETTING DIRECTION

"The future you see is the future you get."
- Robert Allen

As the NEW CEO of your business, you're responsible for making important decisions, and one of those decisions is to establish the future direction of your company. You do this by coming up with a crystal-clear mental picture or vision of what you want your company to become in the future, clarifying your mission for achieving your vision, and defining your company core values to define the type of behavior that's acceptable throughout the process. Together, these three tasks can help you define the future direction of your company.

Once you complete these tasks, you'll be able to share your vision, mission, and company core values with all of your employees and use them as a guide for developing strategies, goals, and action plans. This helps brings everyone in the organization into alignment and is essential for building a healthy company culture.

CHAPTER 5

CREATE YOUR IDEAL BUSINESS VISION

*"Good business leaders create a vision, articulate
the vision, passionately own the vision, and
relentlessly drive it to completion."*
- Jack Welch

If you were to time-travel to some point in the future, what would your business be like? When you looked around, what would you expect to see? Would you be jumping for joy because your business experienced rapid growth and record sales? Would you be elated because your business is now insanely profitable, having expanded into new locations or territories? Would you be feeling grateful because your income doubled and you now have more time to spend with your family and to take vacations? Do you have more free time now to do other fun and meaningful things in your life? What exactly would you expect to see? More importantly, what do you want to see?

DESIGN YOUR FUTURE TODAY

I once heard that defining what you're after is 50 percent of the battle to get there, and I totally believe it. In the early years of my business, I was too consumed with the day-to-day business operations to be concerned about my business future. Instead of taking time to dream about future possibilities, I spent my time experimenting with the latest marketing technique, trying to improve my operations, or learning how to deal with employees. My focus was not on the future, but rather on immediate survival. Although the business continued to grow, it wasn't in a focused manner. It wasn't until I sat down and defined what I wanted my business to become that things in my business began to change.

It seems kind of absurd, but can you imagine what it would be like to take a road trip across the country in your car without having in mind any clear idea of where you were heading? You would certainly end up somewhere, but it might not be where you expected. You might take an off-ramp and drive out on an old road that becomes a dead end. You might start to second-guess yourself and even get lost. Imagine the amount of time you would waste. The same thing happens when you don't take the time to define your ideal business vision.

Creating a clear mental picture is one of the most important steps toward making your business dream a reality. Your ideal business vision is a written narrative that provides a clear, concise description of what you want your business to be like in the future, while allowing you to define future goals.

When you take the time to honestly answer some key questions, you'll be able to define the prefect vision for you and your business.

DRAFTING YOUR IDEAL BUSINESS VISION

Drafting your ideal business vision is a creative exercise that's best done in a quiet environment, alone or with your team if you'd like. Set aside a couple hours during which you won't be interrupted. Imagine yourself three to five years into the future. If you want to use a longer time frame, that's perfectly fine. Just be sure your time frame feels realistic to you. A stretch is good, but if it's too unrealistic, you won't really believe it.

You might have to make multiple attempts at writing your ideal business vision before you end up with a copy that satisfies you, but don't let that discourage you. Once you have a version that resonates with you, you can adopt it as your official ideal business vision and share it with your employees. From that point on, every activity you do in your business should help to move you one step closer toward achieving it.

Once finished, your ideal business vision should excite you enough to get you out of bed in the morning, and inspire and motivate you throughout the day. Keep your ideal business vision next to you and refer to it often.

IDEAL BUSINESS VISION NARRATIVE

The first step in writing the ideal business vision is to write out a narrative for how you "see" your business in the future. You can simply answer the questions, or you can actually write it as a story/narrative.

The clearer your ideal business vision is, the closer you are to achieving it. Because this is your vision, there's no wrong or right. As long as it's clear, easily communicated, and exciting to you, you're on the right track.

IDEAL BUSINESS VISION – QUESTIONS

The following are some suggestions for helping you create your own ideal business vision. Use only what seems appropriate and relevant for your particular business. What do you want to see in your ideal business future?

YOUR PRODUCTS & SERVICES

- What types of products or services will you offer in the future?

- How might these change or be enhanced?
- Is there anything you can do to improve performance?
- Will you offer anything new?

Your Ideal Customers

- What types of customers will you target with your products/services?

Your Uniqueness

- What are your core competencies, and how can you use them to build a competitive advantage?
- How will you be positioned in the market?
- What can you do better than your competition?

Your Locations

- How many locations do you have?
- Where are they located?

Your Financials

- What are your annual sales revenues, profit margins, number of transactions, and average transaction amount?

Your Employees

- How many employees do you have?
- How are they dressed, and how do they behave?
- How well do you attract and hire employees?

Your Operations

- How are your operations?
- Does everything function like a well-oiled machine?
- Do you utilize any special technology?

YOUR IMAGE

- What is your image like?
- Has your company received any awards or special recognition?

The following is the first ideal business vision I wrote.

CD CONNECTION
IDEAL BUSINESS VISION – NARRATIVE
CD Connection is a retail store specializing in used entertainment products (CDs, DVDs, VHS, and video games), and a place that allows customers to trade in their unwanted products. With an inventory of 25,000 different items, CD Connection helps customers save money while shopping for current, hard-to-find, out-of-print, and classic older products that look, feel, and perform to the highest quality standards.

By December 2003, CD Connection will firmly establish itself as a household name in Thurston County, Washington. CD Connection will be voted "The Best CD Store of South Sound" in the Daily Olympians annual survey. Through our Lacey, Washington, location, with 12 knowledgeable employees, we will experience annual sales of $853,000 with a net profit margin of 24 percent.

CD Connection will acquire and retain long-term relationships within our target market, which currently consists of 60 percent male and 40 percent female customers, primarily between 25 and 55 years of age.

CD Connection will position itself in the market to compete by stressing exceptional quality at a great value. Our use of décor, memorabilia, and new technologies will reinforce our value, quality, and satisfaction we provide our customers.

All products at CD Connection go through multiple inspections, function as they are supposed to, and are guaranteed against defects.

Employees of CD Connection are easily identified with their clean appearance, uniform, and name tag. They will always provide exemplary customer service by greeting the customer when they enter and leave the store, and by providing fast, efficient service.

A systematic process of business development will be implemented to realize our ideal business vision. All systems in the business will be fully documented, paving the way for future expansion. Our processes for how we operate and what the customer experiences will be consistent. All employees will know what is expected of them and how they contribute to the success of our business. They enjoy working at the CD Connection.

IDEAL BUSINESS VISION – KEY MEASURABLES

Once you've drafted your ideal business vision narrative, the next step is to define any key measurables that can be used as targets or objectives for developing your strategies. In addition to annual sales revenue and profit margin, write down what you consider to be your key measurables.

FINANCIAL OBJECTIVES

- Sales Revenues: $853,000
- Profit Margin: 24%

KEY MEASURABLES

- 25,000 SKU Inventory
- Voted "The Best CD Store of South Sound"
- 12 Key Employees
- Companywide Documented Processes Implemented
- Technology over Competition
- Unbeatable Guarantee

SOMETIMES LESS IS MORE

The ideal business vision narrative is a clear, concise, detailed description of your future business. That level of detail helps you define your key measurables for which you can build strategies, but there are other times when a short statement will suffice. The ideal business vision statement is a vision narrative that's been reduced to a short, concise, easy-to-remember statement that's simpler to communicate to your staff. To test its effectiveness, regularly ask team members what your vision is. If it's too complicated, they won't remember it.

The following are some examples of short vision statements:

Disney: To make people happy
IKEA: To create a better everyday life for the many people
Microsoft: Empower people through great software anytime, anyplace, and on any device

KEY POINTS

- Your ideal business vision is what you want your business to become in the next three to five years—or longer if you want.
- Your ideal business vision contains a narrative, which describes the look and feel of your ideal business, in detail, over the next three to five years.

- Your ideal business vision defines your financial objectives and key measurables used to create your ideal business vision.

- To make your ideal business vison easier for employees to remember, you can adopt a short vision statement.

ACTION STEPS

1. Write your ideal business vision narrative; include partners or members of your staff if you'd like. Find a quiet location in which you won't be interrupted.

2. Define your financial objectives and key measurables.

CHAPTER 6

IDENTIFY YOUR CORE VALUES

*"Focus on making choices to lead your
life that aligns with your core values in
the most purposeful way possible."*
- Roy T. Bennett

Company core values are the principles and beliefs that guide you and your employees as you conduct your daily business. Identifying your company core values is important because it helps build the foundation that defines who you are, where you're going, how you're going to get there, and when. If you don't take the time to define and communicate your company core values, you're far more likely to experience issues that can limit your overall growth.

I often encounter resistance when trying to convince business owners of the importance of core values. I remember a business owner who believed it was pointless to define and communicate core values because he believed his employees were already aware of them. He felt this was common sense that everyone should know. He couldn't have been more wrong. When the core values were finally defined, it became obvious who in the company didn't share the same values.

Taking the time to define and communicate your company core values is beneficial to your company in the following ways.

CORE VALUES HELP YOU HIRE THE RIGHT PEOPLE

I used to struggle with hiring employees. I wanted to be sure I was hiring the right types of employees. I was often attracted to a specific personality type and their previous work experience. I had no idea how identifying core values would have made the hiring process much easier.

Not every company is a right fit for every employee. You want to hire the people who exhibit the traits, attributes, and beliefs that you want to be the norm for your culture. Incorporating your company core values is important to your hiring process.

Your company core values help you attract and retain employees that share your values. It's one thing to match the skills with an applicant, but it's another thing to make sure the person you're hiring is a true fit for your company. It's hard to detect whether an applicant has the same company core values unless you ask specific questions that can draw them out of the applicant.

CORE VALUES PLAYING CARDS

I know a company that uses a special set of core-values playing cards every time they interview a job candidate. Each card in the deck has a different core value listed on it. When preparing for the interview, the five cards that contain the actual company core values are removed from the deck. Next they pull an additional five other random cards out of the deck for total of ten cards. During the interview process, they ask the applicant to look at the ten cards and pick their own top 5 core values that are most important to them. If the applicant chooses the cards that match the company core-values, then they believe the applicant is a good fit for potential employment. If non-matching values cards are picked, then the applicant is not considered for employment. This is a quick way to see if the applicant shares the same company core values. To get your own set of core values playing cards, visit www.cleaningbusinessbuilders.com.

When you have employees who don't embrace your company core values, their actions hurt your company more than their skills can help it. How many times have you kept an employee because they were skilled at the work they did, even though their attitude was so tough to deal with? Weeding out these types of individuals is like a breath of fresh air. The weight is lifted off your shoulders, and you immediately feel better.

Don't sacrifice your company core values for any one individual. It's not worth it.

CORE VALUES HELP YOU MAKE KEY DECISIONS

In addition to the guidance your company core values offer with hiring decisions, they also help you make critical decisions in all other areas of your business. They can help you evaluate priorities, establish goals, and set company direction. Refer to your company core values every time you're faced with a major business decision. Do they past the values test?

CORE VALUES HELP CREATE BRAND IDENTITY AND A COMPANY CULTURE

Your company core values define your company's character and brand. Not only do they help you attract the right type of employees, they also help you attract customers that share your same values. Oftentimes people want to buy from local companies because they value supporting the local small business owners, or they support companies that they know value sustainable practices. Likes attract likes, and friends like to buy from friends.

When you have clearly defined core values that are embraced and communicated throughout your whole company, they will attract customers that follow the same values. When creating your company core values, think about how you want your business to be seen and how you want to stand out. What kind of people do you want to appeal to that share the same beliefs as you?

SEPARATING YOURSELF FROM YOUR COMPETITION

Company core values separate you from your competitors: what's important to your business may be completely different from what's important to your competition. Perhaps you value quality and going the extra mile, but your competitor values speed and urgency. Not only do your core values set you apart from every other competitor, they also attract the customers who share your values. What do you value most? What does "better" mean to your business when comparing yourself to your competitors?

DEFINING YOUR COMPANY CORE VALUES

If you haven't taken the time to define your core values, or if it's been a while since you looked at the ones you have, it might be the perfect time to re-examine them to make sure they're serving you. Every company should have defined company core values, and if you don't, you should create them!

Involve your employees or management in the creation of your company core values by surveying the entire company to get a feel for what they believe in, what they think are the most important aspects of your business, and what they love about coming to work every day. Ask them to write down what they feel are the company's guiding principles and beliefs. (Sometimes these are positive traits they identify in key people.) You can then gather all their responses and vote on which ones to adopt.

EXAMPLES OF COMPANY CORE VALUES

Here are some examples of core values from which you may wish to choose:

- Fun-loving
- Having integrity
- Motivated
- Positive
- Optimistic
- Honest
- Efficient
- Innovative
- Creative
- Humorous
- Inspiring
- Passionate
- Respectful
- Athletic
- Fit
- Courageous
- Educated
- Respected
- Loving
- Nurturing
- Reliable
- Loyal
- Committed
- Open-minded
- Consistent

WELL-KNOWN COMPANY CORE VALUES

IKEA
Leadership by example
Constant desire for renewal
Humbleness and willpower
Striving to meet reality

Accept and delegate responsibility
Simplicity
Constantly being "on the way"
Daring to be different
Togetherness and enthusiasm
Cost-consciousness

FACEBOOK
Be bold
Focus on impact
Move fast
Be open
Build social value

ACCENTURE
Stewardship
Best people
Client value creation
One global network
Respect for the individual
Integrity

NIKE – THE "11 MAXIMS"
It is our nature to innovate.
Nike is a company.
Nike is a brand.
Simplify and go.
The consumer decides.
Be a sponge.
Evolve immediately.
Do the right thing.
Master the fundamentals.
We are on the offense – always.
Remember the man (the late Bill Bowerman, Nike co-founder)

KEY POINTS

- Company core values are the principles and beliefs that guide you and your employees as you conduct your daily business.

- Core values help you hire the right people and can help prevent you from making costly hiring mistakes.

- Core values help you make key decisions by making sure all decisions are in alignment with what is most important for the company.

- Core values help define your company culture by getting all your people on the same page.

ACTION STEPS

1. Identify your company core values. If you have a management team, have them help you to identify the principles and beliefs that guide your company on a daily basis.

CHAPTER 7

UNDERSTAND YOUR MISSION

*"Outstanding people have one thing in
common: An absolute sense of mission."*
- Zig Ziglar

Now that you've identified your company core values, the next step is to become very clear about why you're in business in the first place. If we don't take time to clarify our "why," we often take on things that seem like a good idea at the time but aren't really in the best interest of the company. The easiest way to clarify your why is by drafting a mission statement. If you already have one, perhaps it's time to revisit it to see if it still holds true for you.

Your mission statement, in its simplest form, should be your **statement of purpose that guides your daily activities**. It's your summary of what your company does. Your mission provides the guiding direction for developing your strategy, searching out new opportunities, and allocating your company resources that lead you to your ideal business vision. It communicates to everyone who you come in contact with how you plan to reach your ideal business vision.

Your mission statement is built on your company core values that you communicate to your staff, customers, and vendors. Your mission statement can help you maintain focus and prevent you from going off in some other direction, making it harder to get distracted.

You can establish your mission by thinking about your ideal business vision and answering these two questions: **"What business are we in?"** and **"Why will customers buy this product or service?"**

STAYING FOCUSED

Being very clear about your purpose can help you avoid getting distracted by shiny objects—the things that distract us from what we're supposed to be doing. Being reminded of your mission helps you stay focused. Your core values, mission, and vision all work together to keep you on track.

Your company mission should be as concise as possible. A mission statement that takes several paragraphs to explain is likely to be confusing or misunderstood. If other people have difficulty understanding the essence of your business purpose, it will probably have to be redone.

You mission statement should also be in alignment with your personal version of success.

EXAMPLES OF MISSION STATEMENTS

Here are some examples of company mission statements that vary in the way they're written. Ben & Jerry's has three mission statements that guide their decision-making: a product mission, an economic mission, and a social mission.

Ben & Jerry's Product Mission Statement

To make, distribute and sell the finest quality all natural ice cream and euphoric concoctions with a continued commitment to incorporating wholesome, natural ingredients and promoting business practices that respect the Earth and the Environment.

1. After reading Ben & Jerry's mission statement, can you tell what business they are in? Absolutely, they're in the ice-cream business.

2. Does it answer why people would buy their product? Yes, people want fine-quality, all-natural ice cream with euphoric concoctions.

3. Does it communicate their core values? Yes, it does. This statement expresses that Ben & Jerry's will use natural ingredients while promoting business practices that are friendly to our Earth and environment.

Advanced Auto Parts, Inc.

It is the Mission of Advance Auto Parts to provide personal vehicle owners and enthusiasts with the vehicle related products and knowledge that fulfill their wants and needs at the right price. Our friendly, knowledgeable and professional staff will help inspire, educate and problem-solve for our customers.

1. After reading this company's mission statement, see if you can determine what business they are in, why customers would buy from them, and what their core values are.

Drafting your own mission statement

Now it's time to draft your own company mission statement. This process will help you reaffirm the purpose of your business and your core values. This process usually takes several attempts, so relax and have fun with this process. When you're satisfied with your statement, ask a friend or colleague to read it and have them explain back to you the purpose of your business. When this is accomplished, you'll be able to clearly communicate what you're doing and why you're doing it.

SIMPLE MISSION STATEMENT DRAFT

The following is a template that can be used to create a simple mission statement. Once you fill out this template, feel free to draft your mission statements using words that feel comfortable for you expressing your purpose. Have fun with this!

_____provides_____
Your Business   *Products or Services*

for_____. _____
         Description of Your Customers   *Your Business*

stands for_____, _____, _____,
              Core Values

and will conduct business according to these values.

KEY POINTS

- Your mission statement is a statement of purpose that guides your daily activities.
- Your mission statement is built on your company core values, which can be communicated to your staff, customers, vendors, and potential investors.
- Your mission statement can help keep you focused. It will be harder to get distracted.

- Your mission statement answers two critical questions: "What business are we in?" and "Why will customers buy this product or service?"

ACTION STEPS

1. Draft a copy of your mission statement for your company.

MODULE THREE:

TOOLS FOR ORGANIZING YOUR WORK

"For every minute spent organizing, an hour is earned."
- Benjamin Franklin

Now that you've taken the time to set the future direction of your company by defining your ideal business vision, clarifying your company core values, and committing to your mission, it's time to put together a strategy that can help you reach it.

It's time to organize your business in a way that helps you get far more done with less effort, become much more effective, and get the chaos under control. When your work is organized and everybody knows who is accountable for doing what, employees are happier. You gain a sense of control, and it becomes easier to maintain focus on your ideal business vision.

We accomplish this through the development of company systems. Systems are designed to help you get things done correctly, consistently, and the way you want it to be done in your business.

In this module, you'll define which systems you're going to need to develop for getting your work done, who exactly will be accountable for using the system to do the work, and the set of rules and expectations for how you want the work to be done.

CHAPTER 8

DETERMINE WHAT NEEDS TO BE DONE

"It is not the beauty of a building you should look at; it's the construction of the foundation that will stand the test of time."
- David Allan Coe

Now that you have a much clearer idea of what you want your future business to be, it's time to develop a strategy for reaching your ideal business vision. Wouldn't it be nice if there was a way to know what work needed to be done to help you reach your ideal business vision? A way to keep you focused and on track? A way to monitor your progress as you keep moving forward, and a way to get your whole team involved? Fortunately, there is, and this can all be done by designing your own master systems blueprint.

Your master systems blueprint is a blueprint of all the systems you need to build to help you achieve your ideal business vision. In addition to defining the systems you need, it also enables you to prioritize which ones are the most important, telling you exactly which systems you should be working on at any given time.

WHAT EXACTLY IS A SYSTEM?

You may be wondering what a system is since the word has been used several times already. The word "system" may seem a bit confusing and mysterious, but it's really not that complicated. A system is any type of predetermined procedure, process, method, or course of action designed to consistently achieve a specific result.

If a system is designed and followed the same way each and every time, it will produce the same result over and over again. Systems are often made up of multiple smaller systems, and all work together for the good of the whole larger system.

A car is an example of multiple systems working together for the good of the whole. Within a car are many smaller systems:

- Brake system –produces the result of slowing down and stopping the car
- Electrical system –produces the result of making sure all lights, stereo, instruments, etc. function properly
- Fuel system – produces the result of making the car engine run properly

Each of these smaller "subsystems" functions on its own to produce its own specific results. They work together with the other subsystems, producing one giant overall result—a car that drives and functions as it's supposed to.

For clarification, I often refer to systems, processes, and procedures interchangeably. I know there are some who strictly define *systems*, *processes*, and *procedures*, and if that language suits you better, that's fine. Please use whatever you're most familiar with.

Creating and installing your own systems enables you to bring order and predictability into your business. Without systems, chaos and dysfunction can prevail. However, before you get started, it's important to understand how they can work together in your own business.

THE 5 CRITICAL FOCUS AREAS

In reality, your business is really one giant system made up of many interconnected, smaller subsystems. You can build systems to produce specific results in all areas of your business. If you need to produce a consistent, correct result over and over again, you need to have a system.

When you begin thinking "systemically," it means you developed the ability to think in terms of how all the systems are interconnected with each other. Adopting a systems mindset can enable you to focus on specific areas until you're able to produce the results you're after.

I believe all business systems fit within five specific areas, or subsystems, that produce very specific results necessary for a thriving, prosperous business. I refer to these five areas as the "5 Critical Focus Areas" because they're critical to and necessary for the survival of your business.

The "5 Critical Focus Areas" produce the following results:

1. **Leadership** – to grow your company and guide it toward your ideal business vision
2. **Management** – to get consistent work done in your business without having to do it all yourself
3. **Sales & Marketing** – to get customers that purchase products/services from your business
4. **Operations** – to produce products/services that satisfy your customers
5. **Administration** – to keep your business healthy

As you can see from the illustration below, the "5 Critical Focus Areas" are interconnected subsystems.

THE 5 CRITICAL FOCUS AREAS

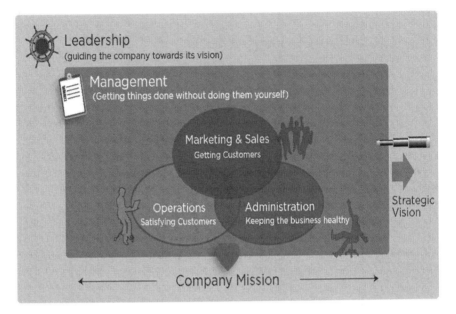

1. Leadership encompasses everything the business does, providing direction and creating a culture that attracts good people. Without effective **leadership,** your business might drift around aimlessly like a ship floating around in the ocean, or driving a car across the country without a clear destination. You're going to end up somewhere, but it may not be where you intended to go.

2. Management provides a structure for getting work done consistently, predictably, and with measured results. Without effective **management,** your business will suffer, work won't get done properly (if it gets done at all), and there's no way to tell how the business is truly performing.

3. Sales and marketing are usually separated into separate functions, however I combine them into one focus area because the result is to get paying customers for the company. Without effective **sales and marketing,**

you won't consistently attract enough prospects or convert them into customers.

4. Operations is what produces the products or delivers the service. Effective operations enable you to deliver products that satisfy your customers and meet their expectations. Without effective **operations,** you risk losing repeat customers.

5. Administration is responsible for the business functions that your customers usually don't see: accounting/ finance, human resources, and IT support are examples. The functions in this focus area are important to the overall health of your company. Without effective **administration,** your business might lack the financial and human resources necessary for continual and sustainable growth.

YOU ARE ONLY AS STRONG AS YOUR WEAKEST LINK

As with any system, you're only as strong as your subsystems. If you were to analyze your "5 Critical Focus Areas," which one would be the weakest? The strongest? No matter how good your business performs within these "5 Critical Focus Areas," you're only as strong as your weakest one. The weakest link could eventually prevent you from growing and achieving your ideal business vision.

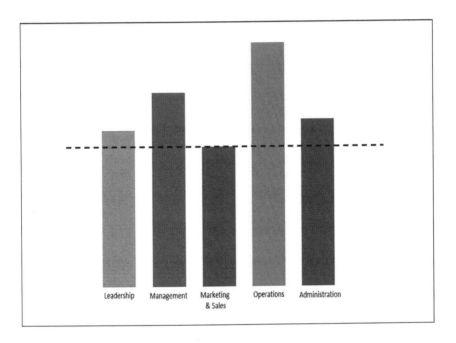

You are only as strong as your weakest link
Where are you focusing your attention?

You may have the greatest sales team in the world, but if your operations are weak and you're not able to produce quality products on a consistent basis, you're going to have problems. Conversely, if you have superb products but no way to sell them, you're not going to get very far either.

SYSTEMS FORM YOUR BUSINESS FOUNDATION

The systems inside each of the "5 Critical Focus Areas" all work together to form the foundation of your business. Just like the foundation supports the weight of the building on top of it, the strength of your business is supported by the foundation you create.

The stronger the foundation, the more your business can grow. Trying to scale your business on a weak foundation is like trying to build a ten-story building on top of a single-story foundation. It's just not going to work. Therefore, it's absolutely vital that you begin strengthening your foundation and building essential systems for your business.

ALIGN YOUR SYSTEMS WITH YOUR IDEAL BUSINESS VISION

The first step toward building the essential systems that can lead your business to your ideal business vision is to be able to identify all the systems used in your business and which ones may still be needed.

Once you create a master list of all the systems your business requires, you can then organize them into a systems blueprint for how your company operates. Next, you can determine which systems deserve your highest priority. You'll always know what systems you should be working on, and you can establish time frames for getting them done. When finished, your master systems blueprint becomes a step-by-step road map for reaching your ideal business vision!

IDENTIFY YOUR CURRENT SYSTEMS

The first step in creating your master systems blueprint is to identify and make a list of all the work you currently do in your business. At first, this may seem overwhelming, but it isn't really that bad. You can do this yourself or ask your employees to write down all the things they do.

EXAMPLE

Here is an example of what your finance system and its subsystems might look like:

FINANCE SYSTEM

Accounts Receivable

- Invoice Customers
- Receive Payments
- Collections

Accounts Payable

- Receive Bills
- Pay Bills
- Tax Reporting

Payroll

- Payroll Reports
- Check Printing

Data Entry and Account Reconciliation

- Reconcile Bank Accounts
- Data Entry
- Accountant Communications

DECIDING WHAT SYSTEMS YOU NEED

In Chapter 3, "Become the "NEW CEO" of Your Business", I asked you to write out all the activities you do in your business. I also asked you to write out a list of different problems that irritate you. You can use these two lists as the starting point for creating your master systems blueprint. The next step is to identify the rest of the key systems that need to be developed. Generally, if you need to produce a consistent result in any area of your business, a system should be developed for it.

Here are a few more guidelines to see if you need to build a system:

1. Do you need a result produced more than one time? Anything that's going to produce only one result does not require a system. If you want your sales team to deliver the same presentation on all their sales calls, then it will need a system.

2. How important is the result? If the result isn't important or critical to you reaching your ideal business vision, then it doesn't make sense to develop a system for it.

3. Do you need predictability and consistency? If so, then it needs a system.

Now that you're ready to begin identifying the essential systems you need, refer to your ideal business vision. Sometimes it's challenging to think about what you're going to need in the future.

CREATING YOUR MASTER SYSTEMS BLUEPRINT

To begin this process of identifying and creating your master business systems blueprint, refer to the following steps:

1. Identify and make a list of all the work that gets done in your business that needs a system to be created.

2. Prioritize the order of what systems should be created first.

Refer to the master systems blueprint worksheet. Earlier I asked you to write out all the activities you do in your business, as well as a list of all the different problems that irritate you. Use these two lists to begin writing down all the systems you need in your business. Next, refer to the 5 Critical Focus Areas. Thinking through each of the 5 Critical Focus Areas can be helpful as you try to identify every system your business needs to reach your ideal business vision.

Continually ask yourself the following question:

"What system is needed to produce/achieve _____ result?"

Prioritize Your Master Systems Blueprint

For this to truly become a blueprint, you have to prioritize the order in which you want your systems to be built. The objectives you set in your ideal business vision determine your priorities. What systems, when fully operational, will provide you with the greatest results? Also, which irritating problems would you like to get rid of once and for all?

Go through your entire master systems blueprint and prioritize all your systems. Even if you have no idea how you're going to build a system, as long as you can identify the result you want, you're on your way toward your ideal business vision!

Key Points

- Your master systems blueprint is a prioritized list of the systems your company needs to do its work that will lead to your reaching the ideal business vision.

- Systems are any type of predetermined procedure, process, method, or course of action that is designed to consistently achieve a specific result. Systems define how the work is to be done.

- Systems are made up of smaller subsystems. The subsystems work together for the good of the whole.

- The 5 Critical Focus Areas are the business subsystems that produce critical results for every business. The 5 Critical Focus Areas are leadership, management, sales and marketing, operations, and administration.

Tool

- Master Systems Blueprint

ACTION STEPS

- Draft your Master Systems Blueprint.

CHAPTER 9

ASSIGN WORK ACCOUNTABILITIES

"If you want to build a ship, don't drum up
people to collect wood and don't assign them
tasks and work, but rather teach them to long
for the endless immensity of the sea."
- Antoine de Saint-Exupery

In the last module we discussed the concept of systemization and how systems are made up of smaller subsystems that all work together for the good of the whole. You were introduced to the 5 Critical Focus Areas, which are critical subsystems required for business success. We also discussed the importance of designing your master systems blueprint, your source to capture and document all the systems you'll need for your business.

In this chapter, you'll learn how to take all the work you just identified on your master systems blueprint and assign it to positions that will be accountable for actually doing the work. By taking the time to plan and organize how all the work was going to get done and who was going to do the work, I found we could actually get work done on time, correctly, and without my direct supervision. In fact, my company was able to continue to function without me being there. True freedom.

THE ORGANIZATION CHART

Most small business owners divide up the work among their employees the best they can as their business grows. Sometimes, employees aren't given a job title, and they aren't sure if they're doing a satisfactory job. They often have no idea what expectations are required of them, and nothing is provided to tell them otherwise. An organization chart helps to address a few of these issues.

Although it may look simple in design, an organization chart is an important, powerful tool to use in your business. Once you've drafted your ideal business vision and master systems blueprint, you're ready to create an organization chart for your company. Setting up an organization chart for your company is essential to getting your business under control. It allows you to take all the work you're currently doing in your business and organize it into actual positions that work together with one another for the overall benefit of your company.

An organization chart provides a graphical representation of how all the work in your business is going to get done and who is responsible for doing the work. By taking some time to sketch out a series of lines and boxes, you can quickly develop a chart that clearly shows all the positions inside your company, which positions are accountable for doing what work, and who each position reports to. It can also show positions you don't currently have but will need to have in order to reach your ideal business vision.

YOUR ORGANIZATION CHART HELPS YOU REACH YOUR IDEAL BUSINESS VISION

It's important to keep your ideal business vision in mind when building your organization chart. Because the ideal business vision is what you want your business to become in the next few years, it makes sense to also include on your organization chart positions you'll need sometime in the future.

Perhaps you know you'll eventually hire a full-time salesperson or a full-time accountant. The planning and anticipating of all future positions should be reflected on your organization chart. This allows your company to be prepared for your future growth while showing everybody in your organization future positions they may eventually want to grow into.

When you take the time to fully develop your organization chart, you're identifying and creating your personnel strategy for reaching your ideal business vision.

BENEFITS OF CREATING AN ORGANIZATION CHART

A well-developed organization chart provides additional benefits as well. It can help your employees understand what their true responsibilities are, or how they and other employees fit into the overall organization.

Often there's little sense of where future advancement opportunities are, as well as confusion and misunderstandings over who is truly responsible for getting specific work done. An organization chart enables everybody in the company to understand all the positions in the company, what every position is accountable for, and how each position contributes to the company achieving its ideal business vision.

ESTABLISHING ORGANIZATION CHART POSITIONS

When creating your organization chart, it's important to establish and assign tasks to job positions instead of individual people. From the time you adopt your organization chart, begin making references to the actual job positions. Over time, employees will come and go, but your positions are likely to remain.

It's a mistake to custom design specific positions for individuals. Often a business owner will create a custom-designed job to match the talents and interests of a particular individual. While this approach may work for a while, when that employee eventually leaves, there will be a gap that might be hard to fill. It may be very challenging to find another person that possesses that exact same set of skills to fill that custom position. If you carefully design your organization chart around positions, you can prevent this type of scenario, making future replacements much easier to find.

Often when a business creates its first organization chart, they identify a few part-time positions that may be assigned to one person. For example, a person may be in charge of sales in addition to maintaining the company website. It's important to refer to each of these as their separate position titles. This establishes the framework that supports the continued growth of the business.

EACH POSITION REPORTS TO ONLY ONE MANAGER

When developing your organization chart, it's important to make sure every identified position reports to only one manager. Oftentimes, when two partners go into business, they split the responsibilities of the business and share the communication with their employees. This often results in both owners acting as the boss of their employees, which can be detrimental to your employees if you're not careful.

I've seen scenarios where one partner will instruct an employee to do something one way, and then the other partner will tell them to do it a different way. It's similar to a child being told different things from each parent. Although it may not be intentional, this type of behavior can be very demoralizing to your employees. Therefore, no position should ever report to more than one manager. Make sure you don't have two (or more) people in charge.

EACH POSITION PRODUCES A SPECIFIC OUTCOME

In addition to having a specific title, each position has to have a clear, specific outcome it's responsible for producing. When you take the time to define the specific outcome for each position, it becomes easier to see how each position fits into the overall organization. The specific outcome is a short description of why the position exists within the organization and provides a method for measuring progress within the position.

Having clearly defined, specific outcomes clarifies what you're paying your employees to do. Each position on the organization chart should have a specific outcome it produces for your company.

Position: Sales Associate
Specific Outcome: *"To convert prospects into satisfied customers so that the needs and financial objectives of the company are met."*

When you have all the specific outcomes that each position is accountable for producing, everyone in the entire business will know how they each contribute to the overall organization.

CREATING YOUR OWN ORGANIZATION CHART

Creating your first organization chart is probably going to take you a few different attempts, so don't be discouraged if you don't get it right the first time.

1. Draw a box at the top for the owner position. Label it "Owner," "President," "CEO," or whatever you want this position to be called.

2. Underneath the Owner/President/CEO box, draw a line down and draw three side-by-side boxes that represent the 3 Core Business Functions, as shown on the 5 Critical Focus Areas illustration. Feel free to rename these functions if you prefer (e.g., using "Service" instead of "Operations").

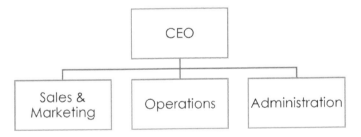

3. Under each of the 3 Core Functions, list the different systems you've identified on your master systems blueprint.

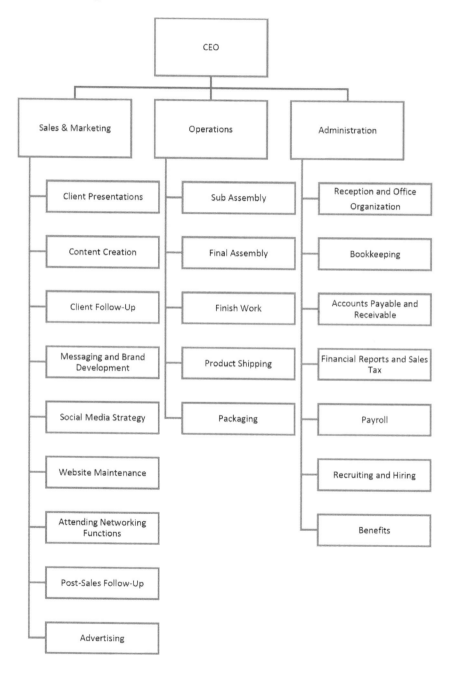

4. Next, begin to think of these 3 Core Functions as three different departments within your company. Under each department are various job positions that are accountable for the systems you previously identified. Assign each system to the most logical job position. Example: Client presentations and client follow up would be assigned to a Sales Associate position. Assign all systems to positions until you have no systems unaccounted for. Refer to your master business systems blueprint to make sure future systems that will lead you to your ideal business vision are accounted for as well.

Sample Organization Chart with Departments and Position Titles

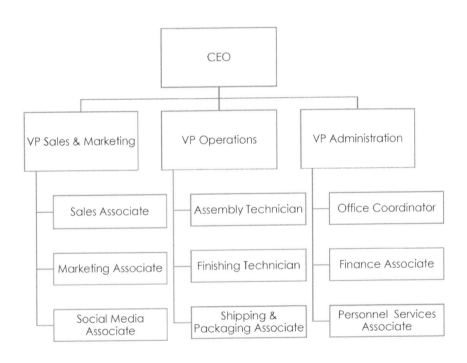

5. Now think about the future positions you'll need under each department and which tasks they'll perform. Remember to identify all systems and positions needed to lead you to your ideal business vision.

ORGANIZATION CHART THAT MATCHES THE IDEAL BUSINESS VISION

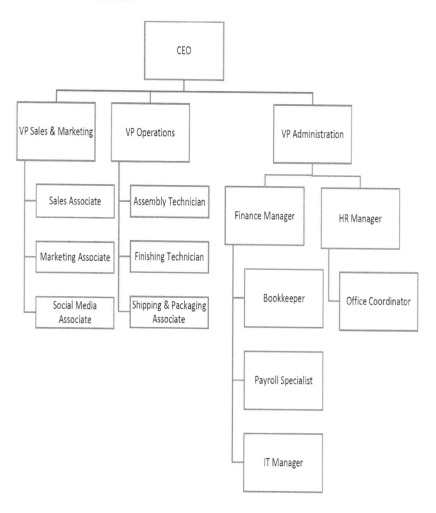

KEY POINTS

- Your organization chart is a tool designed to assign work accountabilities within the entire company. Each position on the chart should have its own title and should be responsible for producing its own specific outcome.
- Your organization chart defines every position and leads you to your ideal business vision. Design it carefully.
- Do not build positions for specific people. Create positions and then find people who have the skills to perform that position.
- Every position in the company can report to only one manager.

TOOL

- Organization Chart Template

ACTION STEPS

- Draft a copy of your company organization chart. Be sure to define the specific outcome each position produces.

CHAPTER 10

CLARIFY EMPLOYEE EXPECTATIONS

*"I've been in this business for a long time, and I
no longer think that anything that I do by way of
clarification is ever going to eradicate the mistakes."*
- Ann Beattie

In the last chapter we discussed the importance of creating an organization chart for your business. The organization chart provides a graphical representation of what work needs to be done and who will be doing the work—work that leads to the achievement of your ideal business vision.

Now that you've learned how to design a blueprint for all the systems your business requires, organize and assign all work to positions on the organization chart, the focus on this chapter is how to clarify expectations with employees in order to establish a positive, successful work environment—an environment in which your employees clearly understand the work they do, how the work is to be done, and the goals and milestones they're supposed to reach. Doing this provides a definition of what success in their job truly looks like.

In addition, supporting and helping your employees get what they want will ultimately help you get what you want. When you create a supportive, positive work environment, you create a place where people actually look forward to coming to work.

HOW TO GET EMPLOYEES TO DO WHAT THEY'RE SUPPOSED TO DO

One of the biggest complaints I hear from business owners is how difficult it can be to get their employees to do what they're supposed to do: they're not doing it correctly, they're sloppy, or they're not doing it at all. Frustrated, these business owners often believe their employees are simply being lazy, they don't care about their job, or they were raised with a poor work ethic.

Whatever the scenario, many of these beliefs come from incorrect assumptions business owners make about their people. I hear these assumptions all the time and have been guilty of making them myself. All too often we assume:

- Employees know what they're supposed to do.
- Employees know how to do what they're supposed to do.
- Employees are going to think like you do.
- Employees know why they do what they're doing, and they should care as much as the owner does.
- Employees will always ask for help if they need it.

In reality, employees don't do what they're supposed to because they don't understand why the work is important in the first place, how they're supposed to do their work, or even what work they should be doing.

EMPLOYEES DON'T UNDERSTAND WHY THEY SHOULD DO THE WORK

When people are being watched or have a supervisor hovering over them, they'll have no problem doing their work. It's when you leave them unsupervised that they often stop working. Since you're working to build a stress-free, sustainable business that can operate without you, that's not an option. You need to find a better way.

Employees need to have a reason to do the work they're doing, and they need to know how the work they're doing fits into the organization. Hurrying to answer a phone by the second ring might seem obsessively nitpicky to some employees. They may ask themselves why such a strict guideline is needed in the first place, and they may believe answering it on the third, fourth, or tenth ring will be good enough.

What they don't realize is that, as a way for your company to develop a competitive advantage over your competition, you promote your company as having exemplary customer service. Clients enjoy and have come to expect the phone to be answered by the second ring. Explaining the "why" behind the reasons your employees should do the things they do puts things in context.

In addition to explaining the "why" behind what they're doing, I also believe it's important to let your employees know exactly what the consequences are if they don't do the work they're supposed to do. I had an employee who refused to wear his new company shirts I designed because he didn't like the color. He would wear the shirt if I was around and take it off when I wasn't around. I had a talk with him and explained the new shirt was an important part of our new brand strategy, and the importance of the image we were working to create with our customers.

One day I went into the office and once again caught the employee not wearing his shirt. I decided it was time to let him know I was done playing games. Either he was going to follow the rules or he wasn't going to have a job. I had our finance person draft up what would be his final paycheck, and then I met with him privately. I let him know I was disappointed that he continued to not wear his company shirt and then handed him his check. I told him he could take the check and we could part ways, or he could start wearing his shirt and I would forget this ever happened.

I could tell by the look in his eye that he wasn't expecting anything like that to happen. He agreed to wear his shirt, and it never became an issue ever again.

When a new employee is hired and before they ever start doing their work, they should learn why they're doing the things they're getting paid to do. By referring them to the organization chart, you can show them how the work they do fits into the big picture.

When employees are provided with a clear explanation as to why something has to be done, or why it has to be done a certain way, the work takes on a whole new meaning. Although the reasons why something needs to be done a specific way may seem really obvious to you, they may not be obvious to the employee.

EMPLOYEES DON'T KNOW HOW TO DO THE WORK

As new employees are hired, most companies do their best to get the employee trained and up to speed as quickly as possible. After all, training costs money and employees are hired to be productive and get work done. The sooner the employee starts working, the better off you are.

However, business owners and managers often make a common mistake: they start their new employees before they're fully trained, assuming their employees know what to do. Then the owners or managers get upset when they realize the employees don't know what they're doing.

Managers often tell their employees what to do and assume that by telling them what to do, they're actually teaching them what to do. Telling and demonstrating are important, but new trainees must practice doing tasks they've been taught before they're turned loose.

If you only tell and demonstrate how to do something, the employee is going to actually start practicing it while on the job—maybe in front of customers or other co-workers—which sets the employee up to fail.

Oftentimes a senior employee is used to train a brand-new employee. Although the senior employee has the experience, they may not be skilled at training. Until the new employee is able to demonstrate that they're proficient at doing a task, they shouldn't be thrown into it unless you consider that their training. Telling people how to do a task isn't the same as effectively training somebody.

THE BROKEN VACUUM CLEANER

I recently spoke with the owner of a residential cleaning company who was complaining to me that one of her employees had a history of breaking the same vacuum cleaner over and over again. It was getting broken when she transported it in a company vehicle. "Why do you think this keeps happening?" I asked. "Because she doesn't care and doesn't respect me or my equipment," she answered.

I then asked her if her employee had ever been properly trained on how to transport a vacuum cleaner in between job sites. "No, I didn't even think anything like that was needed," she replied. "It is if you want your equipment to stop breaking," I replied.

Because employees don't always receive the proper training necessary to perform all the tasks required in their job, sometimes they're hesitant to do the work and are afraid to ask for help.

Employees don't know what they're supposed to do

Another reason an employee doesn't do what they're supposed to do is that they don't know what they're supposed to be doing. There's a big difference between not understanding "how" to do something and not knowing "what" to do. Another variation is that they may know what to do, but may be missing some key information, such as when to start doing something or what the finished project is supposed to look like.

There may also be confusion about what they're supposed to do, which often manifests as "that's not my job." Employees don't know everything they're supposed to do and don't know what success looks like. Expectations need to be spelled out clearly. Don't leave any guesswork.

Employees need to have a clear description of the work for which they're responsible. Sometimes a manager and employee aren't on the same page and have a different understanding of the work they're to be doing. Fortunately, there's a way to address these problems.

A Promise to Do Work

If you've ever hired a contractor, in most cases before the work even begins, you sign some type of contract, which spells out things like the type of work to be performed, when it will be done, and how it will be done. The contract is designed to make sure both parties have a clear understanding of the work to be performed. The contract is really an agreement, a promise of the work to be performed, and in exchange, if the work is done correctly, the contractor gets paid. Both sides get their expectations met, and both sides are happy. If you take the time to draft up your own promise to do work, you, your managers, and your employees can clarify and adopt a set of expectations so that your people can succeed at doing their work.

ESTABLISHING ACCOUNTABILITY

An "Employee Work Agreement" is a document that provides employees with a clear description of the work they were hired to do and the expectations that come with the job. It clearly defines the work for which the employee is accountable, and it gives the employee the opportunity to accept and commit to the accountability. In exchange for the employee's commitment, their manager commits to supporting the employee so that they can succeed at their job. Imagine having that level of commitment in your business. That would be a win-win situation!

When you design an Employee Work Agreement for every position in your company, you no longer have to worry about an employee being unclear about what's expected of them, and you provide them a definition of what success looks like when doing their job.

When I explain the concept of an Employee Work Agreement, most business owners tell me they already have job descriptions. However, there's a big difference between the two.

A job description clearly explains the duties for which an employee is responsible, but there's no accountability or implied mutual support between the employee and their manager. The Employee Work Agreement gives the employee greater clarity on what they're allowed to do in their position and an understanding of what success in their position looks like. They 100 percent understand what they're accountable for. Likewise, managers know exactly what their employees are responsible for. Employee Work Agreements should be given to employees when they're first hired and created for every position on the organization chart.

CONNECTING EVERYONE TO YOUR IDEAL BUSINESS VISION

Employee Work Agreements connect everybody that works in the business together. Each position creates a specific outcome that eventually leads to your ideal business vision. Everybody can do their own work, doubt and uncertainty are eliminated, and employees feel supported. This isn't the case within so many businesses today.

If you decide to create and adopt Employee Work Agreements in your company, they have to be accepted by all. It doesn't work if you have only some of your staff use them. It's either all or nothing.

Because Employee Work Agreements are designed to help a company reach its ideal business vision, they should never be altered or adjusted to meet the needs of any individual. When hired, employees can either accept the terms of the Employee Work Agreement or not accept the position.

One company I know recently implemented Employee Work Agreements in their organization. They had been experiencing some difficulties with one of their key employees and were overlooking his ever-increasing negative attitude because of his skill level. When the owner introduced the Employee Work Agreement to him and asked for his signed commitment to his accountability, he refused to sign it. Clearly this individual wasn't a good fit for the company.

WHAT TO INCLUDE IN AN EMPLOYEE WORK AGREEMENT

There's no one way to make up an Employee Work Agreement, so design one to fit your needs. To be effective, at minimum it should include:

1. **Position Title** – List the title of the position, not an individual's name. You might want to include who

manages this position and if this position manages anybody.

2. **Specific Outcome/Benefits** – What specific outcome should this position produce for your company? How will this position benefit the company? Refer to the position outcomes you defined on the organization chart. Examples might include: "To increase the number of customers for the company," "To make sure all customer orders get shipped correctly and on time," or "To maintain the company website and social media channels to increase the number of leads generated." The specific outcome should be something that can easily be measured.

3. **Work Description** – This is a list of the work for which the position is responsible, leaving no doubt what work this position will do.
   a. "Call on customers, set up appointments, and deliver sales presentations."
   b. "Pack, label, and ship all customer orders."

4. **Expectations** – Work tasks that are expected to be done a specific way should be adequately explained. Expectations can be defined as any standards that should be adhered to when performing the work. "Safety glasses are to be worn at all times" and "Pack, label, and ship all customer orders between 8:00 a.m. and 3:00 p.m." are examples of expectations. Expectations can also include standards of excellence.

5. **Signature Line** – To honor your commitment to this working relationship, the employee and manager should both sign the Employee Work Agreement. Some organizations don't feel right about including signatures. It's as if they're scared they're singing some type of legal document. If either the employee or manager refuse to sign, then perhaps they aren't truly committed to what's written in the document.

EMPLOYEE WORK AGREEMENTS HELP GET WORK DONE

A signed Employee Work Agreement is a major step toward eliminating any confusion and misunderstandings of accountability, providing a greater sense of clarity and a confidence in knowing the work will be performed the way you want it to be performed.

KEY POINTS

- Employee Work Agreements are documents drafted for each job position that clearly explain the work to be performed, who their supervisor is, and expectations for doing the job.

- Employee Work Agreements remove any doubt and ambiguity about their job. They're the "one document" to refer to any time you have an issue with employees.

TOOL

- Employee Work Agreement Template

ACTION STEPS

- Design Employee Work Agreements for every position in the company.

MODULE FOUR:

TOOLS FOR GETTING YOUR WORK DONE

"It's a bad day when you don't get the work done that you need to get done or you don't get it done to the satisfaction"
- David Fincher

Now that you've organized what work is to be done, expectations for how it's to be done, and who will be doing the work, it's now time to discuss getting your work done.

Getting your work done correctly and consistently involves using the right tools and providing a supportive environment in which your people can do their work correctly. Previously we discussed the concept of systemization; in this section we're going to learn how to build systems, which form the foundation for your business. Using systems is the most effective way to get things done.

Getting your work done also includes getting the work done correctly each and every time in the most effective way possible—getting the work done with the least amount of effort, and getting the work done so that you don't have to be the one who does all the work. You can finally take all your hats off, as you begin to conquer the Plateau Effect.

Next, we want to make sure you have tools in place to help you support your employees, not just with their work but also their own personal goals and aspirations. We want to set up a culture where everybody helps each other and everybody wins.

Finally, we're going to discuss the importance of measuring your company's vital signs so that you understand the true performance of your business.

CHAPTER 11

HARNESS THE POWER OF SYSTEMS

*"All systems automated and ready ... A
chimpanzee and two trainees could run her."*
- "Scotty," Star Trek III: The Search for Spock

If you have problems with things being done correctly, things
being missed and slipping through the cracks, or things being
forgotten, you're most likely missing key systems that can
really help you.

In Chapter 8, "Determine What Needs to Be Done," we defined
what systems are. In this chapter we're going to explore
systems in depth so that you can learn to build them for your
own business.

A TOTAL BUSINESS TRANSFORMATION

I can clearly remember how excited I was when I was
introduced to the concept of systemization and what creating
systems could do for me and my business. Learning how to
build and implement them became a real turning point for
me. In fact, systemization completely changed my life as a
business owner and the way I viewed business in general. I

couldn't have gone back to my old ways even if I'd wanted to. I was forever a changed man.

As I began to install various systems in my business, I started to notice many of my irritating problems were going away. It seemed like I had far fewer problems to deal with, and I was able to train employees to perform their work with little or no supervision from me. Employees came to work and knew what to do and what was expected of them. Efficiency improved, and it became easier to monitor how the business was performing. I hired a manager to handle the daily operations, and I was able to take more time away from work—a far cry from the twelve-hour days I worked in the early years.

Because I took the time to design and apply systems within my business, I was able to create a foundation that enabled the business to develop and grow in a healthy, profitable way. However, this certainly didn't happen overnight.

FIND THE ROOT CAUSE OF YOUR PROBLEMS

In Chapter 2, "Take Total Responsibility," we discussed the importance of becoming solution-oriented any time you experience problems. We also discussed how these problems were really opportunities in disguise, opportunities to install systems that might be missing in your business.

"NO, IT'S NOT COMMON SENSE"

One of the biggest mistakes I made as I began to hire employees in the business was to assume these employees knew what to do and what was expected from me. Apparently, I must have thought everybody could read my mind, and when they didn't, I got upset.

"Why did somebody leave this here? ... Isn't this common sense not to do that? ... Why did this get missed?" It didn't really matter what it was; the fact remained that I thought everything should have been common sense, and my employees were just not willing to use theirs or didn't have any in the first place.

I actually hear this a lot from business owners, and they violate this principle on a regular basis. If you want somebody to do something and do it in a certain way, you have to provide instructions and training for doing it this way.

Employees cannot and should not be expected to read your mind. The sooner you understand this, the sooner things will begin to change in your business. From now on, if somebody does something wrong in your business, realize that it's your own fault for not setting up a proper system in the first place.

TRIPPING OVER EMPTY BOXES

There was a situation that used to frustrate me on a regular basis. Employees used our back storeroom to receive merchandise purchased from vendors. Employees would open the boxes, scan in the merchandise, print and attach price labels, and then file the products on the sales floor. They had been trained to do this, and they did it very well.

However, the boxes in which the products arrived would get left behind, lying all over the floor. Whenever I would go into the back room, I would trip over these boxes. This was a constant source of frustration until one day it finally occurred to me that I needed to tweak the system, nothing more.

I immediately reviewed our procedures and realized that nowhere did it mention cutting up and disposing of the boxes. I added this step to the procedures in the reference manual, purchased a new box cutter, and mounted it at the workstation. Next, I trained all staff on this new step and demonstrated how it was to be done.

Amazingly enough, that problem never happened again— no more tripping over empty boxes. Although it may seem complicated, many of the irritating problems we deal with on a daily basis can be easily solved by carefully reviewing the source of the problem.

ADDITIONAL BENEFITS OF SYSTEMIZATION

In addition to allowing you to get organized and work fewer hours, implementing systems in your business can provide the additional following benefits:

SYSTEMS CREATE CONSISTENCY

You expect and deserve to produce consistent results, and that's what your customers expect. Franchises and chain stores use systems because it's the only way to guarantee quality from store to store. If you go into a Starbucks and order a vanilla latte in Seattle, Washington, and then you go into a Starbucks in Washington, DC, the chances are very high that your latte is going to look and taste the same at both locations. Why? Because Starbucks has a system that their employees have been trained to follow that produces a result—a great-tasting vanilla latte. Without systems in place, it can be very difficult to guarantee consistent quality, especially once you begin having multiple employees.

SYSTEMS MAKE IT EASIER TO TRAIN EMPLOYEES

Having defined, documented systems makes it much easier to train employees on how to do the work required of them. Employees need to know that they're doing their work correctly. Providing a documented system to follow leaves little doubt about how work is supposed to be performed.

SYSTEMS CAN BE MEASURED

All systems must have a way to measure how well the work is being performed. Establishing performance measures enables you to track all the activities taking place inside your business, enabling you to make adjustments and improvements along the way. You won't know what needs improving if you don't measure it first.

SYSTEMS ARE REPLICABLE

Once systems are developed, they can be replicated in other locations. Imagine you were going to set up another 100 businesses in various locations around the country. With systems in place, each location can operate exactly the same way. The business becomes dependent on the systems, and it doesn't matter if you're there or not to run the business.

LET'S BAKE A CAKE

To dive a little deeper into a system, we're going to use an example everyone should be able to identify with—a recipe for baking a chocolate cake.

Imagine that you wanted to bake a cake from scratch. The first thing you would probably do is look for a cake recipe. A recipe contains a set of instructions that, when followed, enables you to produce a cake exactly the way the person who created the recipe intended.

Chocolate Cake Recipe

Prep time	Cook time	Total time
15 mins	30 mins	45 mins

Ingredients

- 2 cups all-purpose flour
- 2 cups sugar
- ¾ cup unsweetened cocoa powder
- 2 teaspoons baking powder
- 1½ teaspoons baking soda

- 1 teaspoon salt
- 1 cup milk
- ½ cup vegetable oil
- 2 large eggs
- 2 teaspoons vanilla extract
- 1 cup boiling water
- 1 cup chocolate frosting

Instructions

1. Preheat oven to 350° F. Prepare two 9-inch cake pans by spraying with baking spray or buttering and lightly flouring.

For the chocolate cake:

1. Add flour, sugar, cocoa, baking powder, baking soda, and salt to a large bowl. Stir through flour mixture until combined well.

2. Add milk, vegetable oil, eggs, and vanilla to flour mixture and mix together until well combined. Carefully add boiling water to the cake batter until well combined.

3. Distribute cake batter evenly between the two prepared cake pans. Bake for 30-35 minutes, until a toothpick or cake tester inserted in the center of the chocolate cake comes out clean.

4. Remove from the oven and allow to cool for about 10 minutes, remove from the pan and cool completely.

5. Frost cake with Chocolate Frosting.

The cake recipe also contains a list of all the ingredients you'll need, the precise measurements to use of all the ingredients, the size of the pans you'll need, the temperature at which to bake the cake, and the length of time for baking. If you follow the recipe without changing any of the ingredients, their amounts, the temperature, or the baking time, you'll produce a delicious cake, just like the recipe creator intended. If you alter one or more parts of the recipe, your cake is going to look and taste different. As you can see, as you follow the cake recipe, you're actually following a system. Let's see what this looks like if we map it out.

Chocolate-Cake Baking System

Inputs	Process	Outcome
Ingredients Mixing bowls Measuring spoons Oven	Recipe – containing the steps to follow	Yummy-tasting chocolate cake

Although this is very simplified, you can see all systems have inputs, a process to follow, and a specific outcome that gets produced. Oftentimes people think of a system as just the process and forget some of the other criteria that goes with it.

A system isn't just a checklist to follow. Although systems do contain a sequence of events to be followed in a specific order, there's more to building a system than that.

SYSTEM DESIGN COMPONENTS

Let's explore a little more in depth how you can design systems for your business. If you've never designed a system before, it might take a few attempts before you get the hang of it.

Volumes of articles have been written on system design, including different methodologies. I like to keep things simple so that I can use them. In addition to the inputs, process, and outcome, here are a few more components to fine-tune your systems to use in your business:

1. Name
2. Outcome

3. Inputs

4. Accountability

5. Process

6. Measurement

7. Expectations

Let's examine each one of these in greater detail.

1. NAME
How you want to refer to this system. Use a name that's clear to understand. (Example: Chocolate-Cake Baking System)

2. OUTCOME
The system outcome is the result that's going to be produced by this system. The most important thing to remember here is to make sure this outcome accurately describes what it is you're trying to produce. When you clearly define the specific outcome, it becomes easier to measure the system for effectiveness.
Example:
System Name: Supplies Inventory System
System Outcome: *"To make sure every supply our company needs has been identified and is always in stock in the supply cabinet."*

3. INPUTS
This is where you identify all the various inputs required to operate this system. Inputs are different resources, equipment, and information such as tools, parts, software, safety gear, forms, etc.

4. ACCOUNTABILITY
Every system that's developed in your company must have one position that's responsible for it and the outcome it produces. It's important to note that this may or may not

be the same position that uses the system. The position accountable for a system may be you, the business owner, or a manager in your company.

5. PROCESS

The steps that will be followed to produce the system. Once again using the cake recipe as an example, the process might be something like this:

1. Gather the following list of ingredients.
2. Mix 2 cups of flour, 1 cup of sugar, and 2 eggs in a mixing bowl.
3. Add the rest of the ingredients to the bowl and stir the mixture until you achieve a creamy consistency.
4. Preheat the oven until it reaches 350 degrees.
5. Place pan in the oven.
6. Bake for 30 minutes.
7. Remove from oven and let cool.

Define and write down the work steps that need to be performed to produce the result you wrote down for "System Outcome." Some people prefer drawing boxes in a flow-chart-style diagram to get the correct set of steps that need to be followed.

WHO PERFORMS THE WORK IN THE STEP?

Each step that's been identified in the process needs to be performed by one of the positions in your company. Sometimes some of the steps are performed by different people. Also, some steps have to be performed only after a previous step has already been performed. Determine which position is responsible for performing each step. The same position may do all the steps or different positions may perform selected steps.

WHEN ARE THE STEPS TO BE PERFORMED?

Now that the steps have been defined, when will each step need to be done? In some systems, the steps are performed immediately, one after another, especially if the system is performed by one person.

For other systems, determine and write down when the process steps are to be performed. Do you need additional information from somebody else before you can finish a step? Although in many systems, steps are performed one after the other, there may be days between the performance of steps in other systems.

6. MEASUREMENT
How will you know if the system you created has actually produced the desired outcome you expected? If you don't have any way to measure the success of the system, you really don't know if your system is working. In the cake example, you can visually inspect and taste the cake to see if it was a success.

If your system is designed to produce a vanilla latte, then you can measure how many lattes are produced every hour and each day. You can do periodic spot checks to make sure your quality is what you expect. If you're developing a new customer-service system, you can measure the number of complaints, or in a sales system, you can measure the number of closed sales or orders.

7. EXPECTATIONS
Most companies have a set of expectations regarding how they want the work to be done. These expectations are standards of excellence dictating how you behave and interact with customers, or they're assembly quality standards that need to be followed when producing your products.

Without a clearly defined set of expectations, people using the systems may default to their own expectations. You may even be puzzled, wondering why they would do something a certain way, but unless you spell it out and define it, you run the risk of not being happy with the work result.

Expectations can apply to specific steps within the system or to the overall system.

Examples of expectations:

- Whenever possible, company phones will be answered by the third ring.
- Price tags will always be placed in the upper left-hand corner.
- Gloves will always be worn when performing step 3.
- Purchases over $200 must first be approved by the finance manager.

If someone performs the step but not exactly the way you want it done, check to see if there's an opportunity to add an expectation.

When all done, the system will look like this.

Chocolate-Cake Baking System			
Outcome: To produce a yummy-tasting chocolate cake			
Overall Accountability: Chief Baker			
Inputs	**Process**	**Accountable position**	**Due by:**
Ingredients Mixing bowls Whisk Spoons Oven 2- 9 " cake pans	Add flour, sugar, cocoa, baking powder, baking soda, and salt to a large bowl. Stir through flour mixture until combined well.	Baker	As required
	Add milk, vegetable oil, eggs, and vanilla to flour mixture and mix together until well combined. Carefully add boiling water to the cake batter until well combined		After previous steps are complete
	Distribute cake batter evenly between the two prepared cake pans..		
	Preheat the oven until it reaches 350 degrees.		
	Set timer and bake for 30 minutes		After cake is placed in the oven
	Remove from oven and let cool.		When the timer goes off and a toothpick or cake tester inserted in the center of the chocolate cake comes out clean
	Spread frosting on the cake.		After cake is cool
	Measurement Visually inspect the chocolate cake and taste to make sure it tastes good.		
	Expectations • Allow cake to cool for 10 minutes before putting on frosting. • Always use red and blue sprinkles. • Dishes must be washed and counters cleaned up before eating cake.		

SYSTEMS CRITERIA

To qualify as an actual system in your business, the system should meet the following criteria:

- Systems use various inputs to produce specific outcomes. If you're not concerned about the outcome, there's no reason to design the system.

- The system contains a sequence of steps that must be achieved in order to produce the outcome.

- Systems must be able to be measured to determine their effectiveness.

- Systems contains a clearly defined time frame and sequence for which the steps are to be executed.

- Systems identify specific expectations that must be adhered to when performing a task.

- Systems may be used by multiple positions in a business, but only one position is accountable for the overall results of the system.

TESTING THE SYSTEM FOR EFFECTIVENESS

After a system has been built, the next step is to test it for effectiveness. You don't want to install it as a new system and train your people until you've proven the system will work. As with anything else that's new, it often takes time to realize the full effectiveness of the system. Only after the system has had a chance to prove itself would you then adopt it into your business and create operating instructions for using it.

KEY POINTS

- Systems have the power to transform your business. When designed and implemented correctly, systems produce consistent outcomes, eliminate errors, and improve business performance.

- Systems create consistency, make it easier to train employees, and can be measured to determine their effectiveness.
- Having well-defined systems can greatly free up your time as a business owner, enabling you to do things that really matter to you.
- Systems may be used by multiple positions in a business, but only one position is accountable for the overall results the system produces.

TOOL

- System Design Template

ACTION STEPS

- Begin using the System Design Template and begin creating the first system for your business.

CHAPTER 12

DEVELOP REFERENCE MANUALS

"I hate having to read the manual."
- Trever Horn

In the last chapter we discussed how to create systems, and how implementing them into your business can help you achieve the same level of quality and consistency in everything you do. When your business has systems up and running with people who know how to run them, it's a beautiful thing. Imagine all the different areas of the business working together in harmony.

In this chapter you'll learn how to build reference manuals for each position in your business, reference manuals that help your people know how to work the systems you're paying them to do. Developing a reference guide for each job position provides a way to communicate this important information about your systems to your employees, including all instructions and guidelines for doing their work.

ARE REFERENCE MANUALS REALLY NEEDED?

Every once in a while I encounter somebody who's struggling to use a certain feature on one of their electronic devices:

"How do I get it to do this?" or "What does this mean?" or "I didn't know it could do this!" Although they could have answered all of those questions if they had taken the time to read the owner's manual, the fact is they didn't.

Very few people will actually sit down and read an owner's manual before using the product, whether it's a phone, an appliance, or a new car. However, can you imagine what might happen if they did? Having a full understanding of how to use all the features might dramatically change their experience using the product. Instead of having to call somebody to help them figure something out, they might be empowered to take care of it on their own.

What if your employees had an owner's manual for the job they're performing, and what if they read and understood the manual—a manual that had all the rules and instructions for the results they were expected to produce—before beginning their position? Imagine if they could find answers and fix things on their own without always having to ask for help.

A reference manual is like an owner's manual for a position. It clearly explains how you want things to be done in the job and the company. It provides a way to communicate a lot of information while giving your people the independence and security they need.

One time, one of my employees had to take a leave of absence, and I temporarily had to do their job, a job that I had created years earlier and used to do myself. When I started to perform the tasks, I realized I had absolutely no clue what I was doing. Fortunately, reference manuals had been created for each position. After taking a quick glance at the manual, I was able to perform the required tasks correctly. I didn't have to ask for help, and having the reference manual made all the difference for me.

WHY LEAVE ANYTHING TO CHANCE?

Often there's a lot of resistance to creating reference manuals, especially for each of your positions, because of the time involved in creating them. However, when you take the time to spell out the policies and processes of your business, you prevent your employees from making up their own rules and essentially designing their own jobs.

ADVANTAGES OF HAVING REFERENCE MANUALS

There are also other benefits to building reference manuals for your business that are often overlooked.

CREATING UNIFORMITY

Reference manuals help ensure all employees are on the same page and further clarify expectations, create a sense of order, and provide stability.

What an eye-opening experience it was to realize that I was the cause of so much of the frustration I experienced because I hadn't taken the time to clearly define, document, and train my employees on what and how I wanted things to be done.

If I had an expectation that my employees would perform tasks the way I wanted them to, I had to be very clear and define exactly what and how I wanted things done, and by what set of standards. I learned not to leave anything to chance, not even the smallest detail. If you don't provide clear instructions, you're expecting your employees to read your mind. Instructions can provide them a way to find answers and fix things on their own without always having to ask for help.

However, so many business owners still hire employees and let them start doing their jobs before they're properly trained, and they often lack any type of a reference manual for the new employee to use. Even if a reference manual does exist, the chances are the new employee either doesn't know about it or doesn't know how to use it.

HELPS TRAIN YOUR PEOPLE

Having reference manuals means that important information that your employees need to know—such as system instructions, checklists, etc.—is all in one place.

When new employees are hired, there's often pressure to get them up and running in their job as soon as possible. Not all companies have a training program in place, and creating reference manuals can make the new transition easier. Upon hire, new employees should be provided a reference manual for the job they're doing.

A training checklist can be included containing each specific task the employee will be performing; once an employee demonstrates proficiency in that task, it can be checked off the list.

Employees in training can be asked to read the reference manual and perform exercises that require them to regularly look up information in the manual. When employees ask specific questions, they should be directed to the manual. The goal is to get all new employees to be familiar with the reference manual and to refer to it often.

MAXIMIZING THE VALUE OF YOUR BUSINESS

Having documented reference manuals for all your systems adds additional value to your business. Imagine a potential buyer who's looking at your business and someone else's business. Your business is fully systemized with operations manuals, while the other business is not. Which business do you think is going to be more appealing?

At the time I sold my business, having a complete set of documented reference manuals made the difference to my buyer that allowed me to see the business at a premium. Having documented systems that can help a new buyer transition to becoming the owner brings in a higher perceived value. A business without documented systems in place has a lower perceived value; the business assets are often limited in value.

Maximize your business value. Show that you have value and pride in your business. Show that you have invested your time wisely and were dedicated to your team to make sure they always knew what to do.

PROTECT YOUR PERSONAL TIME

If your employees call you during your personal time, you have a problem. You need to have manuals, policies, and systems in place. There is never a reason that should justify bothering you during your personal time. If your office burns down, you should have insurance. You can be called when you return to work.

That may sound extreme, but there is truth to it. I used to be called multiple times on my day off until one day I realized I didn't like it. I returned to work and called a team meeting. "From now on, you're no longer allowed to call me on my day off!" I said. The look of horror on my employees' faces told me that they were scared. "What do you mean we can't call you?" one of them asked. "You heard me," I said. "I hired you all because you're intelligent people. If you have a problem, figure it out. I trust you. If you screw up, I'll know you made the best decision you could make, and I'll help to make sure you keep learning."

Less than a year later, I took my first two-week vacation since opening the business ten years earlier. I did not call to see how things were going, and nobody called me. When I returned, to my amazement my team had record sales. There were no issues and everything went okay. I think my team wanted to prove to me how well they could perform in my absence, and they did an excellent job.

If you don't allow your employees to learn and develop without you, they'll always depend on you. Make sure when you train your people you're training them to be truly independent; when doing your training, provide scenarios and problems in which they're required to refer to the reference manual. Make them learn how to look up the information they need. How else are they going to learn? If you don't do this, they'll pick up the phone and call you.

CHOOSE THE FORMAT YOU LIKE

Not all operations manuals are the same, and it's important that you adopt a format that you like and will use. Although most people think of using notebook binders when it comes to operations manuals, there are other options and hybrids as well. Some companies store all their documentation online, and employees access it through their computer, tablet, or phone. Other companies find it more advantageous to create quick demonstration videos and store them online. No matter what format you use, remember the objective is to make it easy for your employees to access; otherwise, they'll be less likely to use it.

FOCUS ON THE KEY SYSTEMS FIRST

Some business owners think you have to document every tiny detail, which can cause resistance to creating operations manuals, especially for each of your positions, because of the time involved in creating them. Make no mistake: developing training manuals is time-consuming. However, the time it takes to spell out the policies and processes of your business prevents your employees from making up their own rules and designing their own jobs.

When you begin documenting your reference manuals, begin with the key systems used in your business and then progress to the smaller systems. Refer to your master systems blueprint to identify your key systems for each critical function area. The depth of the details included depends on the importance and frequency of the system being documented.

You also don't have to create your reference and training manuals yourself. All my employees helped document our systems and reference manuals. I trained each one of them to capture all the steps they performed on the job, providing each of them a notebook to capture and document the things they were doing. I even gave them the last hour of the day to document. This saved me a lot of time building the reference manuals.

DON'T WORRY ABOUT PERFECTION

It's important to remember that you have to start somewhere. You may be creating the first edition of your operations manuals, which starts with gathering all the current information you have. Include everything you already have, knowing that you'll eventually update and augment it.

WHO IS ACCOUNTABLE FOR KEEPING MANUALS UP-TO-DATE?

You may or may not have thought about this, but somebody has to be accountable for keeping these employee manuals up-to-date. Who's going to be responsible, and is that responsibility listed on your organization chart? When and how often will new updates be created and distributed? What new systems are needed to keep manuals current?

You'll need to address these types of questions as you build your reference manuals. Make sure to determine this in advance of passing them out within your company.

KEY POINTS

- Reference manuals are used to guide employees on how to do certain tasks. Errors are made by missing critical steps, not because an employee doesn't know how to do the job. Therefore, you don't need to spell out every last detail.

- Reference manuals are an important part of your business; they help you communicate with your employees regarding how things are to be done in your business, providing a sense of order and stability to all employees.

- Reference manuals can be used with your company-wide training program.

- Reference manuals provide a means to communicate with your employees on how to perform the tasks of their job.

- Reference manuals improve the value of your business.

- Any company can make reference manuals; however, somebody has to be responsible for keeping them updated.

TOOL

- Reference Manual Template

ACTION STEPS

- Within each of the 5 Critical Focus Areas, construct an outline of your key systems.

- Use your master systems blueprint to create a blueprint for all the systems and subsystems that need to be identified.

- Utilize your people who work the systems to help you document your reference manuals. Remember, sometimes less is more. You aren't writing a novel, but you need enough information to allow somebody to reference it.

- Train your people using the reference guides. Make sure new trainees have to reference these manuals before they can demonstrate proficiency.

Chapter 13

Monitor Your Vital Signs

"What gets measured gets improved."
- Peter Drucker

In the last few chapters we discussed how to structure and be more effective with getting your work done, clarifying expectations with employees, and learning how to best support them. The only way to truly know what's going on in your business is if you're able to effectively measure what's going on in your business.

As you spend each day moving the company toward your ideal business vision, you'll certainly face challenges and issues that could potentially cause you to veer off course. Having the ability to measure your progress along the way will help keep you on track and provide you with the confidence you need to keep moving forward.

Understanding Your Vital Signs

When you go in to see a doctor, whether for a regular checkup or a visit to the emergency room, one of the first things that happens is the measuring of your vital signs.

Vital signs are measurements of the human body's most basic and essential functions; they provide critical information about a patient's state of heath. The four main vital signs are:

- Body temperature
- Pulse rate
- Respiration rate
- Blood pressure

By measuring vital signs, medical professionals can:

1. Identify the existence of an acute medical problem
2. Quantify the magnitude of a particular illness

Through the regular monitoring of these vital signs, potential medical problems can be detected in advance, and the same is true with your business. Your business has its own set of vital signs that need to be measured on a regular basis. If you don't regularly monitor the vital signs of your own business, you're going to have a difficult time making decisions and understanding the progress you're making. You may focus your time and energy in the wrong areas, areas that you think are important but may not be leading you to making progress toward reaching your ideal business vision.

As the NEW CEO, it's your responsibility to make sure you're making progress toward achieving your ideal business vision. That's just one of the benefits you'll get from monitoring your company's vital signs. Another benefit is gaining a clear understanding of what's currently working and not working, what can and should be improved, and how your employees are performing. Until you have a way to measure every specific area of your business, it's nearly impossible to make any kind of long-lasting improvement. Before you can start monitoring your own company's vital signs, you have to understand what they are.

IDENTIFYING YOUR COMPANY'S VITAL SIGNS

The vital signs of your business are a set of indicators that you monitor so you can assess the critical areas of your business. Every area of business has specific indicators that should be monitored. Refer to the 5 Critical Focus Areas.

Once you determine the most important indicators for you to measure, you can begin tracking the overall performance of your business. Although indicators are often called by different names, I refer to two different types of indicators that make up your company's vital signs: success indicators and performance indicators.

SUCCESS INDICATORS

Success indicators enable you to monitor and see how your business as a whole is progressing toward reaching your ideal business vision. I refer to these as "success indicators" because of the importance of reaching your ideal business vision. These success indicators are a few key items that require only a quick glance to assess if you're still on track. When you drafted your ideal business vision narrative, you defined several key measurables. Now you need to create indicators for these key measurables.

EXAMPLES OF SUCCESS INDICATORS

The following is an example of success indicators that were identified in the ideal business vision (see page on ideal business vision).

FINANCIAL OBJECTIVES
- *Sales Revenues:* $853,000
- *Profit Margin:* 24%

KEY MEASURABLES

- *25,000 SKU Inventory*
- *Voted "The Best of South Sound"*
- *12 Key Employees*
- *Companywide Documented Processes Implemented*
- *Technology over Competition*

Performance Indicators

The other type of indicators that make up your company's vital signs are performance indicators that enable you to monitor and manage the performance within the major functions of your business.

The performance indicators you choose to monitor depend on the type of business you have and the industry you're in. The key is to identify the indicator that will be the most useful and provide you with relevant data that you can use. It does no good to track indicators if they're not going to help you make decisions in some way.

Once you've decided on which indicators to track, you can begin monitoring and reviewing them on a regular basis.

Examples of Performance Indicators

The following are examples of performance indicators you can track in your business. Identify the indicators that will provide you with the most relevant, useful data about your company.

- Number of Sales
- Number of Transactions
- Average Sale Amount
- Amount of Foot Traffic
- Number of Website Visitors

- Number of Appointments Set
- Sales Conversion Rate
- Number of Units Produced
- Inventory Levels
- Customer Satisfaction Level
- Number of Returns
- Personnel Costs
- Average Lead Time
- Average Turnaround Time
- Number of Telephone Inquiries

COLLECTING THE DATA TO MEASURE

After you've determined what indicators you want to track, you need to figure out how to get this information. Some of the indicator data will be easy to gather because it's readily available on your financial statements, point-of-sale software, or your website analytics. For other types of data that aren't readily available in an existing report, you'll have to find additional ways to collect it.

This may require you to be creative and develop your own systems for collecting the rest of the information. For example, if you determine that tracking the number of complaints is an important indicator for you to monitor in order to improve performance, how will you track them? When will you track them, and who's going to be responsible for tracking them? Sometimes all that's required are a pencil and paper to create a tick chart. Not all systems have to be high-tech or complicated. What's important is that the information is consistently tracked over time.

When developing your own system for collecting indicator data, consider these six areas:

1. What source(s) are available for gathering indicator data?
2. How often should the data be collected?
3. When should the data be collected?
4. Who will be accountable for collecting this data?
5. What steps should be followed for collecting the data?
6. Does a new system need to be developed to collect the data?

When I finally realized the importance of measuring indicators in my company, one of the first things I wanted to track was customer foot traffic. I wanted to be able to track not only how many people came into the store each day, but also the number and percentage of customers who were actually making purchases. At first, I wasn't sure how I could go about collecting that data, but I eventually developed a system that could.

I purchased a simple motion detector, similar to the kind you see on the bottom of an electronic garage-door opener. The detector shot a beam of light across to a reflector, and whenever anything broke through the light beam, a buzzer went off. By replacing the buzzer with an incremental number counter, I was able to count how many people walked through the door.

The counts from the motion detector weren't accurate because, when a customer walked in the door and eventually left through the door, the counter would read "two." In addition, I also had to account for employees, delivery people, and other random folks that would stop in that were not actually customers.

To remove these non-customer people from consideration, I came up with the following formula.

(Door Counter / 2) – (Door Counter / 2) x 15%
(544 / 2) – (544 / 2 x 15%) = 41
272 – 41 = 231 Customers
Using 15 percent for non-customers was an educated guess that I used the entire time.

CUSTOMER FOOT-TRAFFIC COUNTING SYSTEM

Here is how the system worked and what it looked like when it was up and running.

Customer Foot-Traffic Counting System	
System outcome	To measure how many customers come into the store each day
Indicator data source	Motion sensor with door counter
When the data is collected	Every night
Who collects the data	Closing shift manager
Steps to follow	1. End of shift – write down door-counter number on the customer foot-traffic worksheet. 2. Reset the counter to zero to prepare for next day. 3. Update traffic counts into the "Foot Traffic" spreadsheet. 4. Spreadsheet uses formula to remove non-customer numbers. 5. Add final number to the monthly "Vital Signs Report."

After identifying all the indicators you want to monitor and then creating the systems for collecting the data, you'll want to create a place to store them for review. There are many ways to do this that range from customized, sophisticated dashboards using graphs and charts to simple spreadsheets. To get you started, the "Vital Signs Tracking Sheet" will work just fine.

Vital Signs Tracking Sheet

Use this worksheet as an example for creating a dashboard for your company. Start small and track indicators as you go.

Company Vital Signs					
Who	Month	Target Result	Previous Period	Current Period	Progress
	Success Indicators				
	Sales	$53,000	$49,942	$51,330	+$1,398
	Profit Margin	24%	18%	19%	+1%
	# of Employees	12	8	8	-
	Inventory Level	24,000	18,000	18,563	+ 563
	Performance Indicators				
	Average Transaction Amount	$50	$37.85	$40.98	+$3.13
	# of Customers	420	395	410	+15
	% Lead Conversion Rate	45%	32%	35%	+3%

Reviewing and Analyzing What You Measured

After collecting the data, your final step is to review and analyze what you track on a regular basis. It does no good to go through the trouble of collecting indicator data if you're never going to analyze and do anything with them.

What really helped me to remember to analyze my data consistently was when I set up time for reviewing my indicators as a recurring appointment on my calendar. I had a specific date and time reserved specifically every month for reviewing my indicators. I used a very simple spreadsheet to track my vital signs from month to month, so it became easy to spot trends and verify my progress. By scheduling these appointments in advance, I was able to develop the habit for always staying up-to-date.

As the NEW CEO of your company, it's your responsibility to review and analyze your vital signs. Here are some suggestions for building this discipline into your CEO responsibilities:

1. Start small – If measuring data is new to you, choose and build your data-collection systems one at a time. Don't overwhelm yourself by measuring everything all at once.

2. Create a routine – Choose a specific date and time each month that you reserve specifically for reviewing your performance-tracking metrics, preferably the same time and day each month.

3. Keep it simple – It's the data that's important, not the look and feel of it. You can increase the sophistication of creating a dashboard as time permits.

MEASURING PUTS YOU IN CONTROL

In the beginning, I spent many years operating my business with my head in the sand, so learning how to measure my important indicators was a turning point for me in my business.

Once I learned what to track and started doing so on a consistent basis, my business performance began to increase, along with a renewed feeling of being in control. If you're willing to take the time to establish and track your own indicators, I'm confident the outcome will be the same for you.

Management guru Peter Drucker said, "What gets measured gets improved," and that sums it up best. The only way to know if you're making progress toward reaching your ideal business vision and making improvements in your business is by monitoring your vital signs on a consistent basis. Start gathering and tracking your data to help you confidently make decisions in your business. Goodbye, ostrich business owner!

KEY POINTS

- Just as doctors monitor your vital signs to see how healthy you are, your business has vital signs that have to be monitored as well.

- Your vital signs provide insights into how your business is performing and what things you can do to make improvements.

- If you don't measure your vital signs, you can never make improvements to your business.

- Vital signs are indicators, and all businesses have common indicators, although you may have indicators specific to your business.

- Track your indicators on a regular basis, and keep aware of trends.

TOOL

- Vital Signs Worksheet

ACTION STEPS

- Review the list of possible indicators and determine the ones you want to track in your business and what system(s) will be required to gather the required data.

- Determine who will be responsible for gathering the data.

CHAPTER 14

IMPROVE EMPLOYEE RELATIONSHIPS

*"It is literally true that you can succeed best
and quickest by helping others to succeed."*
- Napoleon Hill

Now that we've discussed the importance of systems, using reference manuals, and monitoring your vital signs, we're going to focus this chapter on supporting your people doing the work, more specifically, on how to keep your employees happy and engaged so that they continue to be successful and productive and do great work for you.

HELPING YOUR EMPLOYEES ACHIEVE WHAT THEY WANT

I think it's easy to understand that if our employees are happy and like what they do, they're going to be more productive. The question is how do we do that? What can we do to get people to want to do better at their job? I often hear business owners talking about the different things they've tried, attempting to motivate their people. Usually some type of monetary reward is offered, but that doesn't always work because not all people are motivated by the same things.

Zig Ziglar once said, *"You will get all you want in life, if you help enough other people get what they want."* If you take the time to show you care about your employees and to learn what they want, they'll gain a new respect for you. Show them you care. After all, employees are usually your most important resource.

Most business owners never ask what their employees want. Some people think of their employees as "just another body" to do the work. A woman once told me that it took six months for the CEO of the company to stop by and introduce himself after she'd been hired—and the company had only fifteen people! What a way to show you don't care!

We all have inner personal drives and goals that are most important to us. When you create an environment in which you support your employees, you're helping your people reach these innermost desires, and you're creating a place in which people feel valued, respected, and motivated to want to work hard for you. This is completely different from some outside prize to achieve. When was the last time you asked your employees what they want most in their lives? When was the last time you actually showed them you cared for them?

If you want to create a company culture in which everyone in the organization feels supported to be their best and achieve what they truly desire, then a system needs to be created for making this happen. Fortunately, it takes little more than the desire and commitment to making it happen. Setting up a weekly check-in with employee is a quick, effective way to do just that.

The Value of Consistent Check-Ins

One of the best things I ever did was set up a series of weekly check-in meetings with employees that reported directly to me. The weekly check-in meeting is a face-to-face meeting held between a manager and the employees who report directly to them. Once implemented into your company, the weekly check-in meeting can enhance the way you manage your company and dramatically strengthen the relationships with your managers and the people who report to them.

BENEFITS OF WEEKLY CHECK-IN MEETINGS

Taking the time to set up weekly check-in meetings can pay large dividends for your company. Implementing weekly check-in meetings provides the following benefits:

- An opportunity to guide and support your people toward achieving their own version of success

- A chance to support your employees at being their best in the work they do

- A safe place to share thoughts, concerns, problems, or issues; a place in which employees can feel they have your full attention

- A time for employees to discuss the progress of the work they're doing

- A chance for employees to receive guidance and mentoring with specific tasks or situations

- A way to recognize and praise your people

IMPORTANCE OF FEEDBACK FROM MANAGERS

According to psychologists, feedback is one of the most critical requirements for sustained high-level performance. Feedback has an influence on performance, and it's important for your people to know how they're doing. Without appropriate feedback, an employee could be doing something much worse or much better than you think it should be done. They may feel insecure and continually worry if they're doing a good enough job. Managers rarely give performance feedback, and when they do, it's usually much too late, making it not very helpful to the employee. The weekly check-in meetings provide a consistent method of clarifying expectations.

Weekly Check-In Meetings Save Time

You may wonder how you're going to hold weekly meetings in your company if you're short on time. Although some people plan a full hour for these meetings, once you begin holding them, you might find you can get them done in fifteen to twenty minutes. Once you commit to holding these meetings, you'll find they actually save you a lot of time in the long run.

Cutting down on interruptions

One benefit of having weekly check-in meetings is you'll notice over time the number of interruptions drops substantially. Instead of your employees coming to you every time they have a problem or some type of issue, they'll be able to hold it until the meeting.

When managers or employees have questions, they can write them down so that they can be addressed in an efficient manner. This provides a chance to think through the questions before writing them down.

Commit to having Weekly Check-In Meetings

For these weekly check-in meetings to be effective, all your managers must use them. You can't have some of your people holding their meetings and the others not. I've seen this happen, and it really shows who's committed and who isn't. It's easy to dismiss these meetings as being a complete waste of time. However, is it a waste of time to commit to supporting your people so that they can be their very best? Weekly check-in meetings are an investment in your people and your company. Everybody in the company needs to be on board in order to support the long-term success of the business.

YOUR FIRST CHECK-IN MEETING

To make sure your check-in meetings get off to a good start, be sure to plan your first meeting in advance. Your employees may be wondering why you want to meet with them in the first place. They may think they did something wrong and feel anxious. If you establish clear expectations in the beginning, you can pave the way for a successful relationship.

DISCUSS THE GROUND RULES

It's important to begin the meeting with a discussion of the ground rules. Tell your employees what they can expect from you. You can tell them to expect these meetings to be a safe zone in which they can share work issues or challenges they might normally be afraid to talk about. You'll tell them how they're doing in their job and provide feedback for any improvements they can make.

Tell your employees what you expect from them. Don't assume that they know. Ask your employees what they need from you in order to be the most effective at their jobs. This will help establish your relationship as a manager who cares.

ALWAYS USE A WEEKLY CHECK-IN MEETING AGENDA

During your weekly check-in meetings, always use an agenda. In fact, I think it's a good idea to provide your employees with the agenda the day before the meeting takes place. You and your employees can add items to the agenda during the week.

Some things to include in your meeting agenda are:

1. Identify the key objectives of the meeting. Send your employees a copy of the agenda a day or two before the meeting so that they'll know what the meeting objectives are.

2. Review ongoing work. This is where you can discuss the ongoing work that's taking place, including updates and reports. You should be genuinely interested in how your employees are doing and how to best support them.

3. Identify and resolve any work or personal issues. Also, "issues" doesn't mean they're automatically negative.

4. Discuss company news. Discuss any new policies, procedures, or important news relevant to your employees.

5. Include carry-over items. These are items you didn't get to that you're doing to hold over until next meeting.

KEY POINTS

- We can be successful and get what we want if we're willing to help other people be successful and get what they want.

- People aren't motivated by the same things. Find out what is most important to your employees.

- Weekly check-in meetings provide a way to support employees on a consistent basis and establish your company culture as one that really cares and supports its employees.

- All managers in your company should hold weekly check-in meetings with their direct reports or they won't be effective. It's either all or nothing.

TOOL
- Weekly Meeting Agenda

ACTION STEPS
- Create a weekly check-in meeting agenda for managers to use when they hold their meetings.

- Communicate with your managers and train them on how to hold weekly check-in meetings with their employees.
- Hold your first meeting with your management team.

PUTTING IT ALL TOGETHER

It's now time to take everything we discussed in the previous fourteen chapters and put it all together so that you can implement these tools in your business. Although the tools discussed throughout this book are quite simple in nature, they can be challenging at times to implement. They take time to put into place, and results won't happen overnight; however, it will be worth it.

By gaining clarity, you've identified the things that might be holding you back from achieving the success you deserve. You're becoming the NEW CEO and shifting your work priorities from working IN your business to working ON your business. You're becoming a strategic leader committed to transforming your business.

When you perform the foundational work, you become clear about your ideal business vision and about your company core values and mission, providing you a precise target at which to aim and the filters to keep you aligned with your personal version of success.

With your ideal business vision clearly defined, you can identify, organize, and assign to staff the work it's going to take to reach that vision. Assigning accountabilities and clarifying expectations will go a long way toward creating a successful culture in which employees will enjoy coming to work.

Once you've organized the work, it's time to get the work done. By defining effective systems, proper documentation, and a way to measure the work performance, more work will be done with much less effort.

These final chapters are to help you implement the changes needed to transform your business. You must take care when bringing these new tools and ideas into your business; not everybody will react positively to the changes you're making, especially somebody who isn't used to being judged on their performance.

Finally, the last chapter will let you know how we can help you if you want assistance implementing these changes.

CHAPTER 15

EMBRACE THE CHANGE

"Progress is impossible without change,
and those who cannot change their
minds cannot change anything."
- George Bernard Shaw

Change can be scary and unsettling for many people. We all get used to doing things a certain way and having things done a certain way. We create expectations in our minds for the way things are supposed to be and the way things are supposed to happen. When something unexpected happens or we have to deviate from the norm, we begin to feel uncomfortable. This uncomfortable feeling can be so strong that oftentimes people are unwilling to go ahead and make the change.

If you've gone through the exercises in this book, you've worked hard to define your new ideal business vision and identify the systems your company needs to reach that vision. You've developed a graphical chart of your entire company, complete with new position titles, the work each position is responsible for doing, and the outcomes they're to produce.

You learned the importance of employee work agreements and the part they play in creating healthy relationships between managers and employees, relationships built on trust and mutual respect. You understand how monitor your company's vital signs so that you know how to start making improvements.

Now it's time to get your team members involved. This chapter deals with the best way to bring about the change and to inform your people of the changes you're making in a way that won't leave them feeling fearful.

COMMUNICATING CHANGE WITH YOUR TEAM

Chances are, several of your team members already know that you've been working on the changes you're making with your business. However, it's likely that not everyone is aware of what's been going on, and eventually you're going to have to start involving these team members as well.

Although you may be excited and enthusiastic about sharing your ideal business vision with your employees, you must be careful when you explain the changes you're going to be making and how exactly you plan to implement these changes. You want to make sure your employees are all on board with you; you don't want to freak them out. How do you do that?

In 2000, I decided to purchase a small local company that I thought had great potential. The company had downsized, and by the time I was ready to make the purchase, there was only one key employee left who understood the entire operations of the company. Although I had talked to this employee several times and was assured everything was okay, the minute the sale was final and I took possession of the keys, the employee quit. I learned later he was so fearful of any changes I might make that he felt safer quitting.

Although there are a number of different ways to communicate change within your organization, the easiest method seems to be holding a series of company meetings specifically designed to address the change that's happening.

THE BUSINESS ROLLOUT MEETING

The easiest way to inform and educate your employees about the changes you're making in your business is to sit down with them in a company meeting. This isn't an ordinary company meeting; this meeting is designed for you to share your vision and how the company is going to be organized in order to reach the vision.

The minute you mention organization chart, or re-org, ears will perk up. Chances are, somebody in your company has gone through a re-org, and it might not have been a pleasant experience. However, through careful planning and preparation, you can anticipate any apprehension.

Hopefully your people will be excited about what you're going to share with them. This meeting is a chance for you to create excitement and positive expectations about what's to come in the company.

MEET INDIVIDUALLY WITH SPECIFIC INDIVIDUALS

It's a good idea to think about any individuals who might be impacted by the proposed changes and to meet privately with them before your company rollout meeting—especially if you believe somebody might have an adverse reaction to what you're going to say. You don't want somebody getting upset and throwing a fit during your meeting.

If your new organization chart shows individuals taking on more (or fewer) accountabilities, you should talk to them in advance. If you expect somebody might react negatively to the changes you're proposing—somebody who will have fewer accountabilities or somebody who will be reporting to a new manager—you definitely want to talk with them in advance. If you plan to promote somebody and increase their accountabilities, still talk with them. They may not want to be promoted.

If somebody refuses to accept the proposed changes you're making, it might be time to part ways. You've worked hard to design and organize your new business structure to reach your ideal business vision. You can't have people who are unwilling to change ruin it for the rest of your company.

HOLDING THE BUSINESS ROLLOUT MEETINGS

Once you decide to hold your first business rollout meeting, let your employees know a few weeks in advance. When you hold your first rollout meeting, carefully go through the changes you plan to make in your company, starting with your ideal business vision and moving on to your organization chart. Let your team know that you're going to be focusing your attention working ON your business instead of IN your business. Let them know that you're going to be developing systems, and you're going to need their help.

Most important of all, give them a chance to ask questions. They'll most likely have quite a few of them. If you take the time to carefully plan this first meeting, you can get your entire company involved and willing to help reach your ideal business vision.

After your first meeting is over, you might want to hold a "State of the Company" meeting once per quarter to maintain the momentum with your employees. This way everyone will look forward to hearing about the latest changes and learn about the progress the company is making toward reaching its ideal business vision.

FEAR OF GIVING UP CONTROL

Your employees aren't the only ones who may have a difficult time embracing change. As you begin to implement the changes in your growing business, you may find it difficult to give up control of some of the key tasks you're used to doing. You've probably spent years doing things your way and might have even adopted the mind-set that you're the only one who can perform a particular task or service at a certain level of quality and expertise. (Sure, other people can do the tasks but not the same way you do and not with the same level of care.) As the business owner, you've grown and developed your business from the ground up. It's your baby. The thought of somebody else taking over and doing your work can be very frightening, which is why so many business owners struggle with growth.

No matter how good and skilled your employees may be, it may still be difficult to imagine them doing the work you do. One business owner started working with me because he was starting to plan for his eventual retirement. We worked together to reorganize his company, and when we were developing his organization chart, he had no desire to relinquish control of any of the positions that were assigned to him. Even though he wanted more time off to spend with his family, the thought of relinquishing control of certain tasks terrified him.

He kept trying to convince me that nobody else could ever do his job because he'd made it up from the very beginning. However, without being willing to transition someone new into the position, he was going to have a tough time.

Now this doesn't mean that you'll be haphazardly throwing somebody into the position to do the work you used to do. You'll have somebody who's trained and understands the position, someone who will perform the work for you.

Your well-designed systems will enable your employees to produce consistent results while you get to manage how well these results are being produced. You then have the option to adjust the system until the desired results are achieved each and every time.

SOME PEOPLE WILL RESIST CHANGE

Keep in mind that a few people will likely resist the changes you want to make. If you find somebody who seems unwilling to make changes, ask them why. See if you can figure out why they feel that way. In most cases, these people are more concerned about what's in their best interest, not the company's.

Chances are, if there are some of these people in your company, you're probably already aware of who they are. You just haven't wanted to admit it. The time will come when you part ways, and again, that's best for everybody. The people who leave are destined for something more in alignment with what they really want. You're doing them a favor in the long run, and it's better to let these people go now instead of later.

CHANGE TAKES TIME BUT IT'S WORTH IT

Going through this process of transforming and reorganizing your business takes time. The larger your company, the longer it's going to take. Similar to a large ocean liner attempting to make a turn, it takes a long time. The principles are fairly simple to grasp and understand, but it takes work to make the changes and implement them. Anything worth doing is worth doing well, so take your time and keep focused, making the changes you need.

The transformation I experienced was well worth the effort I put into it. Once you begin making these changes, you'll begin experiencing the changes yourself. Although subtle at first, you'll soon realize that things are working better. Your stress level will go down, and you'll no longer be pulled in every direction.

Embrace the change, knowing that it's leading to a better business and a better life for you and your family. These principles worked for me, and I know they'll work for you. To your success!

KEY POINTS

- Change is required to transform your business. Expect to step out of your comfort zone to help move your business forward.

- Your people might not be as enthusiastic as you are toward the change you're making, and some might actually resist. This could lead to parting ways with some of your employees.

- A business rollout meeting is an effective way to communicate your changes with your entire staff.

- Before having your meeting, meet privately with any individuals who might react negatively.

- It can be scary and difficult to give up tasks you've done for a long time; however, giving up control is the only way to grow and free yourself from your business.

TOOL

- Business Roll Out Meeting Agenda

ACTION STEPS

- Prepare a meeting to communicate the changes you plan to make in your company. Create an agenda and prepare for the meeting. Gather everything you need, and then hold your meeting.

- Make a list of those tasks over which you're afraid to give up control. Is the fear real or imagined? What safeguards can be put into place to eliminate this fear?

How will NOT overcoming this fear hold you back and prevent you from reaching your ideal business vision?

CHAPTER 16

NEXT STEPS

There you have it—a system to help you eliminate stress, work fewer hours, and be more profitable in your business.

I hope you have enjoyed reading about the Systems Advantage™, and learning the strategies and tools you can implement to allow you to keep growing towards your ideal business vision. My sincere hope and desire is that you will take the time to study them in order to grasp their significance.

Although they are fairly easy to understand, these tools can at times be challenging to implement into your company culture. However, with dedication and practice you will become more confident with your ability to use them, and be able to witness firsthand some of the immediate benefits. Performance and communications will improve, and many of the problems and frustrations you're accustomed to will fade away. Your business will forever change, and you will forever be a changed business owner.

If you believe you are ready and committed to making these changes outlined in this book into your business, please visit www.DarylMurrow.com for additional resources to assist you with this process.

If you have any questions, comments, or feedback in general or about the material, or if you would like additional assistance implementing these tools into your business please contact me. I am happy to help.

To Your Success,

Daryl Murrow

About the Author

Daryl Murrow is an author, business coach, speaker and entrepreneur. He launched his first business in 1990 at the age of twenty-five and has owned businesses in service, retail, and manufacturing.

After getting caught in the plateau effect and experiencing the stress, frustration, and chaos that came with growing a business, Daryl searched to find the root cause of all his problems. His discovery led to a total transformation of his business. Frustrations in his business disappeared, performance improved, and the amount of free time he enjoyed dramatically increased.

In 2008, Daryl sold his retail business and became a business coach to spread awareness and educate overwhelmed business owners who launched their business without prior experience. He has since personally coached and provided training to thousands of business clients.

When Daryl isn't working, he enjoys spending time outdoors in the great Pacific Northwest with his wife, Raquel, and his two sons, Joe and Andrew.

About the Author's Work

If you're caught in the plateau effect, and feel frustrated, stressed out, and overwhelmed with the growth of your business, then it's time to take back control by learning how to organize, operate, and manage your business in a whole new way—a way that works for you!

Daryl Murrow and his team successfully help small-business CEOs and their management teams implement the Systems Advantage™ Methodology into their companies through the following programs:

- Systems Advantage™ Coaching Programs – Individual and group coaching programs to provide the ongoing education, tools, and support to help your company implement gain the Systems Advantage.

- Systems Advantage™ Consulting – Allow us to do the heavy lifting. We will build, document, and implement your systems for you.

Contact us to schedule a 30 minute, no-obligation meeting to learn how your business can benefit from the Systems Advantage.

Call (360) 358-2072
Email: info@darylmurrow.com
Web: www.darylmurrow.com

Connect with the Author

Website: www.darylmurrow.com

Email: info@darylmurrow.com

Address:
Murrow Group, LLC
PO Box 3017
Lacey, WA 98509

Social Media:

Facebook: fb.me/DarylMurrowCoaching
LinkedIn: www.linkedin.com/in/darylmurrow/
Twitter: @DarylMurrow
Instagram: @daryllmurrow

29651906R00095

Made in the USA
San Bernardino, CA
16 March 2019